My Cat's In Love

FRANK MANOLSON D.V.M.
With the collaboration of
ROBERT C. WILLIAMS D.V.M.

Drawings by
T. A. STEINLEN

My Cat's In Love

Or how to survive your feline's sex life, pregnancy, and kittening

PELHAM BOOKS – LONDON

First published in Great Britain by
PELHAM BOOKS LTD
52 Bedford Square
London, W.C.1
1971

7207 0522 3

Printed in Great Britain by
Tonbridge Printers Ltd,
Peach Hall Works, Tonbridge, Kent, in eleven on twelve point Garamond on paper supplied by P. F. Bingham Ltd and bound by James Burn, Esher, Surrey

Acknowledgements

How are books conceived and born? Many originate in the immaculate minds of lonely authors; this one, I'm afraid, involved an orgy of participants.

The editors in New York suggested that I do a book on the birth of a kitten, a children's picture book, lavishly illustrated with photographs of the actual event, with emphasis on the mystery, the magic, the secrets and lastly the science of feline birth – and in that order.

Bruce Pinkard, photographer, friend and client, had a few hundred shots of Anna, his wife's charismatic Burmese with her litter and without – but none of actual delivery of kittens. We waited for an ideal subject to produce.

Meanwhile, the book was taking shape. I discovered that in fact nowhere between hard covers was the information I needed to round out the facts that I'd learned at college and the practical application I'd learned by experience. At this point another friend, Dr Gordon C. Hard, B.Sc, B.V.Sc, Ph.D, M.R.C.V.S., dug out the relevant research on the subject. And he explained it to me – thank goodness.

Gradually, as I sifted and wrote, the balance of the book changed. The sexual proclivities of the cat needed not a chapter but a section of chapters. That was the obvious beginning. Pregnancy and labour became the middle; the kitten chapters would wind it up. And it was no longer a children's book, nor a picture book. Bruce and I had spent many hours discussing the book. The very title was thought of by him. He said, 'Forget it, man! Let's have a drink!'

And then – with the kitten chapters barely started I became gravely ill. I received letters from many friends. One came from Bob Williams – veterinary college classmate a quarter century ago. Did I need anything, he asked, money, help, or material?

And that's how the kitten chapters got written. How Bob spared time from his busy hospital during the busiest season of the year to send me notes, information, comments and encouragement only he and his family can know, and I will never forget.

And comments and suggestions were coming in thick and fast from my editors across the ocean. I didn't know what the expression 'whipping a book into shape' meant until I started dealing with them. Infuriatingly, the comments and changes were invariably right.

Now the manuscript is in the hands of the real craftsmen of the trade – the printers. During the next six months galley proofs, then page proofs will arrive and cables will fly. And then, a book will be born. It will be a long pregnancy – over two and a half years – and a difficult labour. Be kind to our baby, gentle reader; if you discover imperfections, blame them on me.

Frank Manolson
London
April, 1970

Contents

Part I
THE SEXES

1 The Tomcat

Cats are fastidious creatures. Instinctively they observe the proprieties. They tend to keep their private affairs private. I know, though, that cats that are reared and kept in confined quarters can be as casual as dogs. They have no alternative. One wonders, however, if the things one sees would be different if one didn't see them.

This must be particularly true of sexual behaviour

Most of the published material on the mating of cats is based on observations in catteries, and purebred catteries at that. Generally speaking the stud cat is confined to a cage. The cage may be luxurious. It may be air-conditioned in summer, heated in winter, and part of it may be a huge out-door run. Nevertheless it remains a cage, and the stud cat is a prisoner. If you disagree, open his door and see how many nights he spends at home.

How does the stud system work? The owner of a queen asks the vet., other breeders at a cat show, or the secretary of the local breed society the names of stud-cat owners in the vicinity. Sometimes with rare breeds the stud may be several hours' journey away.

The owner of a superior stud will want to know a great deal about the queen. He won't want his top cat fathering a long line of losers. If the breeder knows what he's doing he won't want his tom to mate its own mother or daughters unless they are particularly outstanding or the purpose is to concentrate a particularly sought-after characteristic. Some breeders don't know and don't care.

If, for example, a mother cat that is slightly spiteful bears a litter that is more than a little spiteful, it would be tempting providence to expect a mating between any two of that family to produce progeny that were all sugar and purrs. Nor would it be entirely unexpected if a completely deaf tom produced slightly deaf daughters when mated to his own mother. In other words, inbreeding intensifies virtues and faults. In the dog world the system has managed to reduce many formerly healthy breeds to exaggerated freaks that are a misery to themselves and a disgrace to those who promulgate them. Now, unhappily, we are beginning to see freak kittens being produced by commercial cat breeders, who are inbreeding the animal to fix such marketable defects as hairlessness and lop ears. Increasingly we are seeing highly neurotic purebreds that are beautiful to look at and impossible to live with.

Even the most commercial of stud-cat owners will want to know about the queen's temperament. If she's known to be spiteful and vicious he will gently suggest that you have her neutered, or go elsewhere. A queen with murder in her heart can do more damage to a stud in sixty seconds than two vets can patch in a week. And vets charge almost as much as stud-cat owners.

If the queen has never been mated before and if the tom is relatively inexperienced, a wise breeder will suggest an older tom.

The stud fee varies from about a third of the price of a kitten up to the full price of a couple of kittens. (A large fee bears no relationship to the tom's performance or virility; it is a reflection of his superior blood lines and the expectation that his kittens will be as good as their father or better.) The price should include a return service if the first doesn't take. Some breeders will refund the price if the queen doesn't bear a litter. It's better to work this out at the beginning, in writing; a couple of months later no one will be able to remember exactly what was agreed.

The queen is almost always taken to the stud. She usually stays a day or two, sometimes three. Her board is usually included in the stud fee.

Many breeders want the queen brought to them as soon as she shows signs of heat. She's probably not receptive during the first day or even two. During this stage she can be introduced to a kennel adjoining the tom's. If she were placed in his kennel immediately on arrival she might claw him to pieces. This is particularly true of virgin queens. After all, they've just been subjected to a journey, a separation from doting owners, and confinement in a strange prison; and (the biggest *and* of all) they don't know what it's all about. From an adjoining kennel, the queen can get used to her surroundings and work up a little healthy curiosity about her next-door neighbour while her body is building up to the event.

A healthy, experienced tom, on the other hand, will mate virtually any queen at any time. He is more confident if he is in familiar territory. If he's not at home he will spend a considerable time investigating the area and staking out his claim, in his own unique manner. First he sniffs about suspiciously. Then he strides about slowly with the stiff stilted gait of a proud matador, and with his buttocks compressed and his tail stretched high he sprays a substance from his anal glands. (I'm sure that the tom thinks it smells rather pleasant and let us hope the queen does too. But although comparatively long stretches of my childhood were spent in stockyards and almost no time at all in perfumed gardens, I find that it stinks.)

The tom has not yet finished laying out his breeding territory. He must then walk about and urinate around its perimeter. That task completed, he makes another circuit, presumably to check that he's done the job thoroughly. Sometimes he may decide to rub his cheeks against an object or surface he hasn't managed to mark. This may be a throwback to a dim evolutionary predecessor which possessed glands in the head. Some grazing animals still do.

These preliminaries are obviously not so vital if the stud is at home, nor are they so prolonged. Although the female may emulate this display it's obviously not as important for her as it is for the male. She appears to be quite content to be mounted in the male's territory. The only home she considers really worth defending is that in which she bears and nurses her young.

Once the stud has the area smelling to his satisfaction he courts the queen. Sometimes ceremony and preliminaries, if they exist, are too subtle for the human eye to see. More often there is a definite courtship. Many species of animals and birds would not consider it a very gallant preliminary. The tom circles around the female. He runs towards her and if she runs away he quickly circles around behind her. As she backs away he may call out to her in a low-pitched but strong tone. This mating call of the male is not at all like the unpleasant threatening sounds we sometimes hear in the night. Those are the signs of rivalry, not love. People who are familiar with the mating call agree that it is a pleasant, reassuring sound. As the male approaches the inexperienced or unready female she may fluff up her coat, draw back her ears, tighten her jaw muscles, and hiss. Those who have been threatened by a cat can confirm that the intention is unmistakable. In this situation the tom, gentleman that he is, makes no attemp to retaliate. He either retreats and awaits a more auspicious moment or he crouches down in a submissive posture. As he cringes he closes his eyes as if to say, 'Do what you like! No matter what you do I shall not strike back.'

If the queen persists in repelling his advances – and one should only give them about ten minutes together – it may mean that she's still too early in the oestral cycle. Most breeders would agree that it's better to separate them and try again a few hours later. If the time is ripe she will respond by crouching, rubbing her face on the ground and sometimes against the male, and she may return his call. She may roll her body (as she does in a normal heat even when no male is about) and she may tread with her feet.

Under laboratory conditions this period of courtship may last only a few seconds or as long as several minutes. In breeding catteries, with doting owners as an alternative distraction, these activities may stretch for as long as an hour.

Copulation in the cat is initiated by the male firmly gripping the neck of the female with his teeth. As he does so the female automatically crouches in the receptive position. That grip obviously makes things easier for the male. It helps him retain his balance. It ensures that without conscious thought he must assume the correct position over the female.*

As the male grabs her the female crouches. While mounted he may rub with his forepaws and the female may tread with hers. He may arch his back and begin pelvic thrusts before his penis becomes erect and before he enters the female. It is then that the female swings her tail to one side and twists her hind end to accommodate the male. Under laboratory conditions this stage of copulation – from the time he grabs her neck and starts thrusting with his pelvis but before he actually inserts his penis – lasts from about one minute to as long as three.

The actual insertion, ejaculation, and separation take less than ten seconds. It's at that stage that the female gives her typical cry, a high-pitched scream quite different from the low-throated response of courtship. As she crics she pulls

* The domestic cat doesn't have a monopoly on this advantageous mannerism; some observers claim that it is practised by all members of the cat family, including the larger species. It would appear to be such an instinctive part of the sexual act for the cat that only with the greatest difficulty can it modify its behaviour in that respect. One scientist had a black-footed cat. This is a wild member of the cat family whose scientific name is *Felis nigripes*. It is much smaller than an ordinary domestic cat. The first few attempts to mate the smaller wild cat to the larger domestic cat were failures, but not through lack of interest on the part of the male or lack of receptivity on the part of the female. The reason the male couldn't consummate the act was that when he grabbed the female by the neck he wasn't long enough to mount her from behind. Only after several attempts did he learn to grab her further back and even after he had learned to modify this action by altering the position backwards, he always had to initiate the act by grabbing at the advanced position on the neck.

ahead and twists towards the male. She does so in order to take a swipe at him.

As the male ejaculates he may make a low sound – halfway between a grunt and a groan – which is usually hardly noticed under the queen's much more penetrating cry. He jumps backwards and may leap several feet to safety. Afterwards, as her nasty streak appears to last only a second or two, he relaxes beside her and grooms himself. He pays particular attention to his penis and to his forepaws. She too grooms herself, paying particular attention to her sexual organs. She may then begin to roll and rub her face against the ground or a surface, and she may attempt to renew the tom's interest by pawing him.

If the cats are allowed to remain together the tom will renew his advances after (many people have timed it with a stop watch) about a minute or so.

Some toms, under laboratory conditions, have been seen to mount a queen ten or a dozen times in a row. As you might expect the intervals lengthen as the marathon progresses. The male becomes more and more interested in the passive moments of post-copulatory grooming. The female, on the other hand, grows more avid with each successive experience.

Cats that have mated in the past appear to develop an attachment for each other, or at least a sort of trust that is normally lacking. The male doesn't leap several feet away because he knows that the female will keep her claws to herself. She will give her typical copulatory cry but then instead of turning on the male she will lie quietly for a moment and then groom herself.

There are of course many other variations on this basic theme. No aspect of life can be too tightly categorized. Some toms, for example, appear to be immune to all the threatening hisses of the female and oblivious to her striking claws. These are usually mature, experienced toms that have been confined to cages and deprived of queens for some months. More of that later.

In a breeding set-up the only aids that man sometimes provides are: (a) a strip of nailed-down matting or carpet to help avoid slipping; (b) a ledge on to which the tom can leap to escape the female after the act is completed; (c) a tranquillizer for a nervous or nasty female; or (d) a trusted human hand to hold a very nervous queen. The latter is rarely used because the human hand, no matter how well trusted and loved, tends to bleed when scratched. It's not that the cat's love suddenly turns to hate. It's just that at that moment some females feel nothing but blind fury. I have no evidence to prove that that's what the cat feels except the fact that the cat strikes out in a paroxysm of claws and teeth. You can interpret that as brotherly love if you like but keep your face away from pussy while you tell her. Not all females act like that. Not even a sizeable majority do. But enough do so that the experienced tom leaps away and the experienced breeder stays out of harm's way during the crucial few seconds while the queen is calming.

Most experienced breeders say that a couple of times are sufficient but some advocate a repeat the following day.

How many queens can a tom handle? This depends very much on the tom. Some virile creatures in the best of health, and on the right side of middle age, can handle a queen a day through the busy four or five months of spring. Even so, such an active tom would probably lose weight and condition.

And some litters might turn out small – say one or two kittens instead of the expected average of four – because of the reduction in numbers of spermatozoa. Many experienced breeders suggest that the average healthy tom should have no more than two or three queens a week, and this accords with common sense.

Young toms in their first post-puberty season and elderly creaky creatures of ten or twelve years might be capable of handling only one a week or even less.

The problem that arises most often with stud cats is not how many queens they can successfuly impregnate but how few they need to keep them happy. Usually the poor tom is miserable because he hasn't had a queen in weeks. Some deprived toms pace up and down like caged lions, some decide to urinate against everything in sight, others try to mount objects, other males, or their keepers. One scientist reported that such activities do not usually lead to ejaculation. Even masturbation with the forepaws is not uncommon.

Some toms just sit in a corner and howl. This piteous cry is given out at irregular intervals and in a staggered rhythm. The human ear simply cannot adjust and accommodate to it as to other background noises, such as a noisy refrigerator. The tom will give out three or four heartrending howls, pause for half a minute, and then howl continuously for fifteen minutes and stop for five. Just as one begins to think he's given up he'll start again. And so it goes – day after day and week after week until the introduction of a queen gives a temporary respite lasting up to a week or ten days.

Queens in heat and lonely cats away from home can and do cry in the same disturbing way. But when the heat is over and the lonely cat is restored to its owners the crying stops. The only thing that can cure the tom is a steady supply of queens, his freedom, or neutering.

Sometimes vets are asked to treat the suffering tom with tranquillizers. This 'solution' should be avoided, however, because while one hears of limited success with such 'nerve' drugs as sparine, acetylpromazine, or chlopromazine, cats can and do react strangely to many of them. Siamese and other Orientals particularly may go quite berserk with them; maybe the drugs remove that bit of acquired inhibition we call domestication. Some vets dispense stilboestrol or one of the other female hormones to counteract the male's sex drive. Aside from the fact that we don't know what long-term side effects those drugs may have, they work only while they're being taken. Stop the drug and the old boy is as miserable as ever.

Stud cats in cages, such as I have been discussing, constitute far less than 1 per cent of tomcats. The rest belong to the vast world of rooftops, alleyways, inaccessible hideaways in warehouses, cellars, and granaries, and sheltered corners of gardens and farmyards. Many of them have homes to go to for rest and food. Contrary to popular belief they are just as affectionate and just as tractable as any other pet cat. And of course they've got that male swagger of confidence that neuters never attain.

There are three main disadvantages to keeping a full tom as a pet. The first is that they don't spend a lot of time at home, especially in the mating season. The second is that they can come home with the most frightful array of scratches, sores, and abscesses, which unless treated can lead to serious complications. The third is that if your pet tom takes it into his head to urinate indoors the whole place will stink for days afterwards. Few odours are quite so penetrating and I have yet to meet anyone who finds this one pleasant. Most find it revolting. And, of course, if you're at all concerned with the problem of homeless strays you must realize that keeping a full tom and allowing him his liberty must add to the problem.

I suspect, however, that the majority of tomcats everywhere (even in this increasingly compartmentalized century) belong to no one. They may have a favourite warehouse or farm or home where they can easily steal or beg, they may have an area that they consider home territory, but in the main they are at home everywhere and nowhere.

Tomcats, whether pets or semi-wild, can cover a fair-sized area and they do. When they hear or smell a queen on heat they'll swoop down on her like Mediterranean beach boys on a foreign blonde. They may have to cross a couple of main roads, climb a fire escape, and traverse a bridge, but they'll find her. As the toms converge on the queen they circle round her, keeping an eye on each other and on the main chance. As one tom moves in, another may attack him. These squabbles produce some of the sounds we hear in the night. During the mêlée a tom slyer or quicker or stronger than the others slants in, mounts the ready queen, and with a quick thrust inseminates her. He rolls off immediately to protect himself either from her or from his fellow toms. As he dismounts another tom is ready to take his place. It is quite normal for even the most sedate feline female to accept several males in turn while she is on heat. The whole business including the preliminary infighting and intercourse with three or four toms can take as little as ten or fifteen minutes if the queen takes fright and dashes home, or it can last the night long.

Certainly everything I've read agrees that the sexual act in the cat is brief – almost cursory. The question that occurs to me is, cats being what they are and labs and catteries being what *they* are, how many natural matings have ever been observed? Just to put it into perspective may I report what two fellow vets tell me they once observed outside the pathology laboratory at the Veterinary College of Sydney University, in Australia.

A tom that used to get his handouts from the lady members of the staff was a common sight in the yard. Early one morning, as one of my two friends wandered into work, he noticed that the tom was mounted on a queen. The cats weren't particularly distracted by his passing and the tom continued his rhythmic thrusts. Later in the morning the other vet arrived in the lab and commented that the tom had found a girlfriend. Later still the two looked out of the window and saw that the cats were still united and thrusting. During the lunchtime exits to the cafeteria the whole staff of the lab passed the cats, which took no notice. And at quitting time that evening the two cats were still strongly united. One of the vets, a dedicated soul, was in the habit of working late into the evening. When he left the lab towards ten o'clock he noticed that the cats were still actively engaged and – believe it or not – when he returned in the morning there they were as if they'd just begun. They continued till lunchtime, when the tom rolled off and the two lay panting and resting for hours in the afternoon sun.

I'm inclined to lay some credence to this story because both my informants are experienced observers and highly regarded vets. Is it possible that this account is closer to the norm than closely observed coitus under laboratory conditions or the necessary briskness of a sexual encounter in the presence of eager rivals? I don't know. And neither does anyone else. I do know that it seems highly doubtful that each and every time they looked out the window they caught the cats just as copulation was beginning. Nor do I think that they are so chauvinistic as to make up such a story in order to impress me and other gullible people with the powers and virility of the Australian male.

Anatomically and physiologically the male cat is similar to other animals. One of the few differences is that his relatively small penis is covered with short sharpish barbs, a bit like the rough covering of a cow's tongue. This tough protective layer doesn't develop if the cat is castrated at an early age. At about three and a half months of age the male hormone starts to form and the growth of spines on the penis is stimulated.

Some texts put the age of puberty at eight months of age. Other observers say that it doesn't occur before eleven or twelve months of age in most toms, and some don't begin breeding until their second spring. They point out that a kitten born in late August of one year would be not quite eight months of age the following spring and it wouldn't be at all unusual for him to skip the sexual activities of the season entirely. The following March or April, however, he would join in enthusiastically. Of course many kittens indulge in sex play as early as four months of age. This may include mounting of objects or fellow kittens or puppies, the typical sexual neck grip, and rhythmic pelvic thrusts. But few kittens, no matter how precocious, successfully enter the female before ten months of age.

At a short distance it is difficult to tell the difference between males and females in a litter of kittens. With maturity, however, the head and shoulders of the male develop and assume the massive strength we associate with the males of many species. His tentative forays into the world become confident night-long circuits as his sexual drives parallel his physical development. Strangely enough, many cats that are castrated after they've had sexual experience will continue to search out the female. And some, despite their sterility, can and do complete sexual union with the queen.

Are all the cries that we hear in the night simply manifestation of the sexual drive? Modern observers think not. Some state that cats stake out their territory and vigorously reject intruders. The tom stakes out his territory by urinating along its outer borders. Others state that much of the noise represents aggression for aggression's sake. It's a bit like the aimless aggression among the lads who look for fights after closing time at the pub.

The queens and the neuters can learn to share our mundane lives and largely to ignore the cries in the night. The tom, though quite willing to be part of a human household, cannot. No creature that shares our lives is so much of the wild.

2 The Neutered Male

NEUTERING – PROS AND CONS

A neutered cat is more likely to settle easily into the routine of an ordered life. He will be quite happy to stay at home in the evening watching television or taking a gentle stroll around the garden. His entire brother, by contrast, has better things to do. Like many active teenage children he will treat the home as a place in which to eat, sleep, and wash between the many exciting adventures obtainable in the great world outside.

Many people have their cats castrated because they believe that after the operation they become more tractable and less aggressive. This is, of course, not always true. Some of the nastiest cats I have known have been neutered males and some of the nicest have been entire toms. The neutered cat, being less active, tends to put on weight and fat creatures are often less liable to bouts of temper. Their good nature may originate in laziness.

Despite all the town and city ordinances many animals urinate, or spray, as it is called, in the most unsuitable places and at the most inconvenient times. They are not out to break the laws. They simply wish to delineate their territory.

Neutered cats once they get the idea appear to relish this activity as much as their un-neutered brothers or sisters. The difference however from the owner's point of view is that the traces of the urine of the neutered animal can usually be erased in less than half an hour's diligent scrubbing. That of the entire male cat is meant to be a permanent reminder of tenure and indeed it usually is. Many people who love cats can reconcile themselves to the odd scrubbing session involved in keeping a neuter but they simply can't cope with that penetrating stench produced by the entire male. They opt for castration.

In all fairness to the entire male one must mention that the vast majority of them restrict their marking activities to the outside perimeter of their territories, which usually means that the home, its porches, its verandahs and its garages are left strictly alone. Few self-respecting cats choose to live in a stench, even one that is self-produced.

Another reason people have their pet cats castrated is that in this increasingly mobile age more and more of us expect to move house. Few young or middle-aged people can say with any degree of certainty that they will be staying in their house for another fifteen years. This is the life span (optimistically) of a cat. The point of this sociological digression is that neutered cats move relatively easily. They may become frightened when you place them in a basket and as a result urinate or defecate. But as I explained earlier, one can generally clean the mess made by a neuter with comparative ease, whereas that made by the entire tom can disrupt the entire journey, whether it's by car, aeroplane, or train. Sometimes there is a transitional period between houses during which the family is forced to live in a hotel or with relatives. The neutered cat may be welcome or at least he can be easily boarded. Few boarding catteries, however, will accept an entire tom. Finally, when the family actually settles into the new home the entire tom may have quite a difficult time establishing his rights in a new neighbourhood. Quite a sizeable number of toms that are brought to veterinary surgeries torn and bleeding from fights have recently been moved. The established neighbourhood toms appear to resent the intrusion of an entire tom far more than they do that of his neutered brother.

One full tom of my acquaintance spent the first eight years of his life in Florida. There in a graceful college town he adorned his owner's home by day and performed valiant services by night. Even in the Deep South nature arranges her seasons so that each and every tom can have a respite of several weeks from his arduous duties. When this tom's owner moved to Massachusetts the breeding season was just ending in Florida and just beginning in New England. The poor tom tried to cope. The combination, however, of the entrenched toms, who resented his move into the area, plus the fascination of a whole neighbourhood of absolutely new females, proved to be his undoing. Some callous observers stated that, by any reckoning, it was a glorious way to die.

A neuter being introduced to a new neighbourhood will also often face a formidable array of strange cats who will immediately wish to assert their superiority. The fights which ensue seldom sound as serious as those in which entire animals are involved, nor is as much damage inflicted. Within a few days those cats near the top of the ladder have moved up a rung and those towards the bottom have moved down a rung and the newcomer has taken his place in between. In those rare incidences in which the neighbourhood cats are really out for blood one must of course confine the stranger indoors for days or even weeks, only letting him out for restricted periods under close supervision. During this introductory period the neighbourhood cats may resent the odour of the newcomer but there is little they can do about it. A few days or weeks later the resentment seems to have lost its edge.

Finally, we must recognize that there are some people who, if it were in their power, would have every male castrated. They would, if they could, not restrict their activities to cats.

Now, what say those who are against the operation? They say, and of course they're right, that it's against nature. One must agree that it is an unnatural operation. So indeed are all operations. So also are the concrete jungles with which man has noisily surrounded himself.

Some people have a more direct and less philosophical approach. They say, quite simply, that the entire tom is a glorious creature, and that of course is also true.

Some people are against neutering tomcats for a reason which may be prosaic or aesthetic, depending on your point of view. These people say that neutered cats put on too much weight, and a fat cat is definitely not a joy to behold. It ceases to be a thing of beauty. The reply to this of course is that there is only one thing that makes animals, or people, fat and that is overeating. Restrict the neuter's intake and he will stay slim, lithe, and beautiful. That, however, is often easier said than done. The neutered cat's main interest in life, in many cases, is eating. If his owner attempts to restrict his intake the simple creature is most unlikely to associate his empty bowl with any kindly motive. His owner, he will conclude, is either being stingy or has suddenly succumbed to that widespread disease called poverty. Even the most coddled home-loving creature, in those circumstances, will soon learn which of the neighbourhood rubbish bins are worth exploring and at which back doors he will get a welcome.

'Oh, that nasty Mrs Smith shouldn't be allowed to keep a cat,' he will be told while the neighbour empties the refrigerator into a soup bowl. 'If she spent less time putting peroxide on her hair and more time looking after her responsibilities she'd be a far nicer woman.'

If cats could talk it would be a far more interesting world.

There is a final and very serious reason that many experienced people give for not having tomcats doctored. The neutered male, they say, is more likely to get urinary blockage due to bladder stones. Wherever cat people gather this subject is debated. Some authorities reply that the reason we see more urinary blockage problems in neutered cats is simply because we see more neutered cats than full toms. If there were as many full toms brought to veterinarians as neuters one might find out in fact that the incidence of urinary blockage was the same in both sorts of male cat... or we might not.

Other authorities claim that it is the cat that is neutered too young that is likely to suffer from this condition. Cats that are not operated on until they are five or six months of age, these authorities feel, are less likely to get urinary blockage. I'll come back to the question of the proper age for the operation in a few moments.

Although it doesn't properly belong in this book I would like to interject here a description of the symptoms of the cat suffering from a urinary blockage. The reason for this unpoetic licence is the hope that a wide dissemination of the description of a very painful condition will lead to its early recognition by even the most ignorant and callous of cat owners. On too many occasions a cat suffers for a day or even two before the owner realizes that it simply must be taken to the veterinarian. Sometimes the condition remains unrecognized. The bladder bursts and the cat dies.

What is it all about? Inside the bladder of some cats there gathers or precipitates a fine sediment, which looks like sand. Some veterinarians call it sand, some gravel; others use the human term and call it stones. Still others, who don't believe that a word is respectable unless it has at least three syllables, call these deposits calculi.

The passage through the middle of the penis of a cat is very fine. It is little thicker than a thick human hair. It doesn't take a very large grain of this material from the bladder to cause an obstruction and then complete blockage. During the early stages, say for a few hours or as much as a day or two, the cat may be able to painfully pass a little bit of urine. But no matter how much pressure it brings to bear the tiny passage, called a urethra, soon becomes completely blocked.

The cat starts out feeling vaguely uncomfortable. He wanders over to his tray or toilet area and strains for two or three or four minutes at a stretch. Then, even if he has passed no urine at all, he goes through the instinctive motions cats use to cover their excreta. He then wanders over to his usual resting place and tries to relax. He may even try to drink a little water or eat food if it's offered. After a few more moments he looks at his abdomen and wonders what's happening. Possibly feeling slightly sheepish, he makes yet another journey to his toilet. There the performance is repeated. After six or maybe thirty-six repetitions the owner may notice that something is wrong. Almost always the inexperienced person will diagnose the condition incorrectly as constipation. He will bring out the oil or milk of magnesia or some form of modified dynamite which he is in the habit of using himself and pour it down the hapless cat's throat. No matter which medicine one uses at this juncture the cat's condition will get progressively worse. Human beings who have suffered a similar stoppage say that it is one of the most painful conditions that they have known. We may assume that the cat suffers equally.

The only possible treatment is professional. The cat must be taken to the veterinarian as soon as possible (not as soon as convenient), no matter what time of the day or night. Because of the great pain involved this is one of those conditions which is always classified as an emergency.

The veterinarian will give the cat a general anaesthetic and then attempt to introduce a very tiny catheter or a tiny needle into the penis and with pressure of water or air attempt to dislodge the offending material. On the first occasion he is almost always successful. After a few days he will discharge the cat, provided it is urinating normally. He may dispense some pills which the cat will be kept on all its days. He may recommend a special diet. He may suggest some additions to the drinking water or sometimes a special source of it.

In my experience almost 50 per cent of cats that once suffered a urinary stoppage due to sand in the bladder suffer a recurrence of the condition a few months or sometimes as long as a couple of years later. One will, of course, have a second go at rectifying the condition. However, if the condition recurs again and again despite all measures most veterinarians recommend euthanasia.

After that long description of a painful condition one may add two further observations to the tomcat versus neutered male controversy. The full tomcat develops a hard scaly cover to the penis as he reaches maturity. This protective coating adds a strength and rigidity to the penis of the full tom which that of his neutered brother does not possess. Moreover, the urethral opening of the tom is usually larger than that of the neuter. Should the full tom suffer a urinary obstruction one can manipulate the penis and introduce catheters or needles with much more ease. Also, one is less likely to injure the delicate tissues underneath.

THE CASTRATION OPERATION AND ITS EFFECTS

The rest of this chapter is devoted simply to the discussion of the actual operation of castration – when it should be done, how it should be arranged, what the owner can do to help both before and after the operation, the possible complications immediately after the operation, and undesirable long-term after effects and what can be done to eliminate them. Those who have already faced this problem with their cats may safely tear these pages out of the book and thus lighten their burden.

Most people obtain a new kitten when it is six or eight or preferably ten or twelve weeks of age. Ninety-five per cent of kittens sold in pet shops are males. This is because male cats are easier to sell. Nature prefers a balance of about 50 per cent male to 50 per cent female, give or take 1 or 2 per cent. She attains this balance by miraculously changing 50 per cent of the pet-shop kittens into females as soon as they reach their new homes.

The wise purchaser makes a detour on the way home. This visit to the veterinarian serves three main purposes.

First, the veterinarian or his assistant will tell you at a glance whether your kitten is a male or a female. If your thickset black-and-white long-haired kitten has been sold to you as a pedigreed Siamese he might charitably point out to you that your kitten is not exactly the best representative of the breed. If the wee creature sits comfortably in the palm of your hand the veterinarian might point out to you that it is probably closer to five or six weeks of age and could not possibly have been properly weaned.

Second, the veterinarian will examine the kitten for the presence of earmites, fleas, lice, ringworm, and other external parasites. Often a thorough dusting of the coat at the veterinarian's *before* the kitten goes home can rid it of fleas and prevent them from getting established in your sofas and carpets. Potbellied kittens may be suffering from internal worms. Appropriate tests may be done or simple pills dispensed at the time. Many newly purchased kittens are suffering from flu. If this disease is recognized in its early stages an injection or two of antibiotics will usually clear it up without complications or after effects. Once entrenched, however, it can easily rage into a bronchitis or a pneumonia. Many cats grow into sickly adults because they had a neglected flu as a kitten. Don't get alarmed, worried, or despondent! The veterinarian can do all three better than you.

Third, the veterinarian can discuss with you such things as inoculations and when they're best given, arrangements for boarding should that become necessary, and exactly how they like to handle their neutering operations.

Most veterinarians must, of necessity, handle all their minor operations on an assembly-line basis. Their methods may appear callous or even heartless to the sentimental owner but like some other things one encounters in life it boils down to a simple matter of economics. The veterinarian and his staff are certainly more than willing to spend several hours or even a whole day with a single case. Few owners, however, are willing or able to pay the fee that would have to be charged for such attention.

The assembly line starts with an appointment. One doesn't want feline patients hanging about a waiting room being frightened by the sights and sounds and odours of strange animals. This is not a case of kindness to animals so much as consideration for human skin. A frightened or nervous cat is more likely to come out of its basket spoiling for blood than one that is resting quietly.

Every good veterinary establishment that I know insists that feline patients coming in for operations must come in a proper cat basket. A proper cat basket is one in which a cat can stretch out or stand up if it wishes. It should be well ventilated without being draughty. It should close securely so that the cat cannot get its foot or its tail or its head out. And ideally it should open at the top, not at the end or the sides. Personally, I prefer the old-fashioned wicker sort, but some of the new plastic ones are not as hideous to the touch as they are to the eye. The vast majority of cats travel easily in baskets. Even those few that resent them at first will usually settle down.

There are of course dozens of alternative methods of transporting a cat. You see them on the ends of leads. You see them clutched in the scratched and torn arms of a bewildered owner who plaintively wails 'It only scratches me when we leave home.' You see cats being optimistically carried in ordinary brown paper bags, or ready for take-off in canvas aeroplane bags. You see them trussed up like calves at a rodeo, but the man is yet to be born who can tie a cat and keep it tied. You see cats in undiscarded potato sacks and in Paris originals.

I once saw a kitten brought into a veterinary surgery in the gentle mouth of a Labrador retriever. 'They go everywhere like that,' the owner explained nonchalantly.

In addition to bringing the kitten in a proper basket and bringing it on time the owner will be asked to ensure that the kitten has not had a mouthful of solid food for at least twelve hours before the operation. In a home with children who may treat any open mouth as a space to be filled this can be no small problem. Often there is only one way to make sure. That is to lock the kitten in an isolated room and ignore its cries. Most kittens, being essentially sensible creatures, will settle down after half an hour or so, and sleep throughout the entire fast. During this period of starvation not even milk is allowed. Some veterinarians, however, will allow water during the first six hours.

Cats must be starved before operations for exactly the same reasons as people who are about to meet their scalpel. It reduces the risk of nausea and sickness.

I know veterinarians still exist in many places who will castrate cats of any age without an anaesthetic. I believe this is wrong. First, it is cruel. British and some American laws now recognize it as such and other countries are following suit. The law states quite simply that any animal whose eyes are open must be given an anaesthetic before undergoing an operation. In the case of larger animals like calves, lambs, and piglets it is often safer and less cruel to use a local anaesthetic. In the cat it is almost always better to administer a general anaesthetic.

There are two other reasons why cats should be anaesthetized. The first is that it is easier on the staff. Where veterinarians insist through ignorance, incompetence, or sheer callousness that the cat should be rolled up in a blanket or stuffed into a rubber boot while they knife it open and wrench out its sexual organs an assistant or assistants almost always end up with an assortment of scars. This sort of veterinarian, I rejoice to say, has practically disappeared from the English-speaking world. One may still run into the odd thick-booted and thicker-mouthed yokel who believes that a measure of human superiority is the volume of protesting cries that can be raised from an animal. In the main, however, such non-doctors of veterinary medicine are to be found only in those countries which border the Mediterranean and in the Far East. Let us hope that they may eventually prove susceptible to the continuing flow of educational material and legislative pressure that emanates from London and New York.

The final reason cats should be given an anaesthetic at this time is that the mental trauma which may be caused by the very rough handling needed to castrate a cat without an anaesthetic could erase weeks or months of kindness. I have known cats that have never recovered from such an experience. At best they remain shy and suspicious for ever more, at worst they become incorrigibly vicious.

What is the best age to have the operation done? Younger kittens are easier to handle. They lose less blood during the operation. They heal quicker and one hopes that they don't remember the whole nasty episode as long as they would if they were older. Not so many years ago two and a half or three months was the most popular age to have the operation done. However, more and more people have noted that kittens altered so young seem to be slightly retarded a month or two later. An additional two to three months of development under the beneficial influence of the testicular hormones make all the difference. Such kittens, it is now thought, develop better bones, stronger necks and heads and shoulders, and above all more robust constitutions and stronger, less fearful characters.

How late can one safely leave the operation? It depends a bit on the time of year. In the depths of a cold winter a five- or six-month-old kitten is unlikely to develop sexually as fast as he would at the height of the breeding season two or three months later. At that time one could quite safely postpone action until seven or seven and a half months of age.

However, I agree with those people who say that five and a half to six and a half months is the ideal age. The kitten has obtained a great deal of benefit from its male hormones but it has not yet developed any overt sexual inclinations. Most sensible people would agree that it is highly unfair to allow a male kitten to just get the idea of sex, with all the attendant psychological changes that that implies, and then with the stroke of a knife remove the whole new world that was just revealing itself to him. Castration of a cat that has never known even vaguely about sex cannot be considered too unkind. Castration of the cat that is aware of maleness, even if he has never experienced the sexual act or even aspired to the conquering battle which precedes it, is more than a simple operation. It is an amputation, albeit a psychological one.

The actual technique of castrating the immature cat is simplicity itself. First, the veterinarian anaesthetizes the kitten. Some do this by introducing the kitten into an anaesthetic bin, a meal box with a couple of inlets for the anaesthetic and oxygen if it is needed. The procedure is safe enough provided one can spare an assistant to sit and watch the kitten every moment of the time in order to remove it the instant anaesthetic depth is reached. Sometimes it sits in the box drooling and panic-stricken for as long as half an hour before the anaesthetic takes effect. Personally I find the method time-wasting for the operators and psychologically disturbing for the kitten. However, every veterinary surgery must keep one of these bins about because there is a small percentage of kittens that cannot be handled in any other way. This percentage rises dramatically if one is dealing with a great many farm or warehouse or stray cats. I have seen some big wildcats, including lions and tigers fresh out of the jungle, that displayed less aggressiveness than some of the so-called domesticated cats that have gone wild in the bomb sites of London or the alleys of New York.

An oxygen mask is a quicker, better method of anaesthetization. An assistant pins the kitten's front legs and neck to the table with one hand and pulls the hind legs out straight with the other, while the veterinarian puts the mask over the kitten's head. This method is quick, safe, and effective, but it involves a certain amount of wrestling. Sometimes a kitten gets its head twisted round and clamps its teeth firmly through one or more digits of the screaming assistant. Sometimes the kitten manages to escape the holder's hands and then everyone rushes around in total panic making sure that all the windows and doors are closed. Those of us who simply can't stand the feeling of suffocation which is often produced by having a mask stuck over one's head will readily sympathize with the kitten's violent attempts to escape.

Another method of inducing sleep in the cat is simple, gentle, and safe provided the whole veterinary establishment is geared to the psychology of the cat. This means that everything must be prepared and ready before the kitten is lifted out of its basket. This is neither complicated nor time consuming. A syringe is filled with sodium pentothal, sometimes known in popular fiction as 'truth serum'. The needle on the syringe must be extremely fine, not thicker than 4/10 or 5/10 of a millimeter. If it's not absolutely sharp it should be thrown away. Beside it lies a pair of curved scissors and a little wad of cotton soaked in alcohol. The table should be thoroughly washed and dried, because often the lingering smell of a preceding patient frightens or upsets the cat that is about to be anaesthetized. Very quietly and gently the veterinarian moves the basket on to the table. Talking in a gentle soothing tone, he opens the basket, strokes the kitten gently around the neck and shoulders, and lifts it out. The assistant grasps the skin of the neck gently but firmly with one hand and extends one front leg forward with the other hand, using the thumb over the elbow to raise the vein below. Meanwhile the veterinarian is using the curved scissors to clip off about an inch or an inch and a half of hair down the front of the leg. He then applies the alcohol swab to the area. He gently inserts the very sharp needle into the vein, which by this time is standing up quite nicely, withdraws the syringe about a quarter of an inch, waits the long second for the blood to come back into the syringe and thus demonstrate that the needle is in fact in the vein, and then nods to the assistant to release the pressure of the thumb, whereupon he slowly injects a cc or two cc's of the anaesthetic.

The trained assistant doesn't release his or her hold. The kitten stares, gulps, generally tastes the anaesthetic and runs its tongue over its lips. A second afterwards the kitten completely relaxes. It slides limply on to its side. The veterinarian pinches a toe and gives a glance at the kitten's eye to determine whether a little bit more anaesthetic should be injected. By this time the assistant is directing his attention to the kitten's scrotum. The hair over the area is trimmed off with scissors or electric clippers and then soaked with antiseptic alcohol. The veterinarian picks a scalpel out of the sterilizer, makes an incision over each testicle, which takes less time than it is taking you to read this sentence, puts the scalpel to the side, grasps the scrotum with one hand, and with the thumb and forefinger of the other firmly pulls the testicle through the opening. He pulls steadily in a straight line and the cords and vessels come through easily. With proper traction they easily break off, leaving the remaining portions safely inside the kitten. The procedure is repeated with the other testicle. Almost never in the younger kitten, of say up to seven months of age, is there any haemorrhage of any consequence afterwards. The kitten is placed back in its basket, comfortably stretched out, but the lid of the basket is not closed until the kitten is actually lifting its head.

The whole procedure, from the time the kitten is first taken out of its basket until it's placed back inside, need take no longer than sixty seconds, provided everyone knows his job and the kitten has not been frightened.

It takes an hour or two or sometimes even longer before the kitten is able to stand properly. Most of them, however, are quite happy to give a little glance at the world through the bars of the basket and sink mercifully back into a deep sleep which can last as long as twelve or even fourteen hours. For this reason when the owners come to collect their kitten they are usually told not to fuss with it. The best thing they can do, they are told, is to place the basket in a quiet, draught-free area of the house and forget it until the following morning. Despite this admonition it is amazing how many times a few short hours later a panic-stricken voice reports on the phone that the kitten has fallen down three flights of stairs.

Each of us, whether animal or human, recovers from anaesthetic in our own individual fashion. I, for example, am the most peaceable of men. I believe the slogan 'Make love not war' is a sensible one because there must come a time in every man's life when he can't do both. (Sadly, I am told that there is a whole new school of literature devoted to describing those who can do neither.) Be that as it may, and it is, a while back I had to have a general anaesthetic. The following day as I was walking down the hospital corridor I encountered the two porters who had wheeled me into the theatre. As is my wont, I showed my teeth at them in what I consider to be a smile and my friends tell me looks like the grimace of an undertaker's cashier.

'Good morning,' said I brightly.

'Hey you, Joe Louis,' replied one. 'D'you still want to fight today?'

The reason I include these highly embarrassing confessions is to illustrate vividly the principle that quite often an anaesthetic, like even the best brands of whisky, can act to lower inhibitions and allow the real personality to emerge. Some experts would say that the cat's normal instinct is to either run away from or claw the stranger. The domestication of the cat is so recent an event that the veneer of amiability hasn't had time to harden properly.

As the kitten wakes from anaesthetic it considers everything within its range of vision as a potential threat. It may try to escape but as its co-ordination is affected even a short jump can be dangerous. More often it decides that everything in its weaving dizzy world must be fought. In simple terms, this means that if you stick your hand into the basket of a cat waking up from an anaesthetic it is quite likely to be scratched into poor quality hamburger. If, as so many owners seem unable to refrain from doing, you actually put your head over the open basket and say 'Poor little Kitty-poo, did the nasty doctor give you a nasty operation?' don't say I didn't warn you if you lose an eye.

May I repeat? The solution to all these problems is the easy one. Stick the basket in a safe place and forget it.

The following morning, open the basket and offer the kitten some breakfast. It will be ravenous. Twenty-four hours is a long time for a kitten to go without food. If its usual breakfast doesn't satisfy it (and it usually won't), you may use the opportunity to introduce it to some food that it has previously refused. Or you can feel all sorry for it and give it an extra egg. Avoid laxative foods like kidney, spleen or raw liver because despite its ravenous appetite the kitten's digestion will be out of kilter for a day or two. Whatever you do don't open the refrigerator and allow the patient carte blanche. A significant proportion of kittens are taken back to the veterinary surgery three or four days after a minor operation because of tummy upsets. Careful questioning reveals that the cause is not the operation or the anaesthetic but overfeeding.

What else can go wrong after the operation? Sometimes at the height of summer the open wound may be invaded by insects. Flies may lay their eggs in it and a few days later they will hatch into maggots. This condition, which many farmers know too well and call flyblow, is always serious and often fatal. If it is impossible for you to keep the kitten behind screened doors and windows until it is completely healed (which may be as long as seven or ten days), you should ask your veterinarian or your chemist for an effective safe repellent.

Sometimes the kitten is so bothered by the incision that it simply will not stop licking the area. It can open a small neat incision into a large gaping wound. If the kitten appears to be constantly returning to the area with its tongue or rubbing the operation site along a rough carpet then you must call your veterinarian. Some veterinarians might suggest that you try a little antibiotic ointment on the area. Most, however, would prefer to see the kitten. Sometimes an injection or two of antibiotic will clear up the condition; sometimes the kitten has to be re-anaesthetized and the area trimmed down to fresh clean tissue.

I must emphasize that only a small fraction of 1 per cent of kittens that are castrated at six months of age or younger develop complications. In one practice which I know they do about forty male kittens a week. Not even two a year go wrong.

Many people ask why veterinarians don't close the incision with two or three stitches. Surely, they say, an open wound is more likely to get infected. This may be true in some parts of the body but it isn't true of the scrotum. Because of its position below the anus it would require a great deal of effort to cleanse the area properly and keep it clean. Then, too, the scrotal skin is particularly sensitive, and the proper cleansing necessary before stitching would probably set up an irritation that the kitten simply could not leave alone. Finally, veterinarians have found over many decades of experience that if the incision is large enough any slight post-operative infection will simply drain away. The scrotum, remember, is near the lowest part of the body.

Sometimes, either because of sloppiness, haste, incompetence, or bad fortune a bit of loose tissue from inside the scrotum is not removed. Even if it protrudes ever so slightly from the incision it may be an avenue through which infection gains access to the body. The kitten will walk stiff-legged. It may lick at the area. More often it will find it too painful to touch. The kitten will go off its food. If you attempt to lift its leg to examine the area it will let you know in no uncertain manner that you are causing pain. Don't try any home remedies. Almost always the kitten must be anaesthetized again, the offending tissue removed, and the surrounding tissues trimmed and cleaned, and of course the animal must be placed on a regime of antibiotics.

That completes the catalogue of woes which may befall the kitten within the first week after the operation. I repeat that any of these mishaps is a very rare occurrence, about one in a thousand. Nevertheless if it happens to be your kitten, that one looms larger than the thousand.

Unfortunately, long-term ill effects associated with castration are more common. Indeed it would be surprising if the removal of an organ which controls such an influential hormone were entirely beneficial. Nature has proved herself very efficient at getting rid of organs that are either inefficient or superfluous. The testicles are neither.

A small percentage of kittens are completely changed by the operation. One occasionally sees kittens that prior to castration were affectionate, curious, and lively and after the operation become blobs. They lose their sparkle and their interest. They sleep and they eat and that's about it. Neither a game nor a hunt nor the passing scene interests them. Fortunately this sort of tragedy is a relative rarity.

A more common effect is that which turns Playful Gus the gourmet into Grabby George the gourmand. My neutered tabby Malcolm is such a cat. Given the opportunity, I believe, he would eat his own weight in meat. My staff call him Malcolm the Horrible and they mean it. The reason they don't like my cat is not just that he's hungry. He's also fast. One only has to put a bag of shopping down for a moment while fumbling for a key and unerringly from within that bag he will fish the only piece of meat and vanish around the corner. This can be amusing the first time it happens. It may even have its funny side a second or a third time, if there is something else to eat stashed away in the refrigerator. But if one has just managed to get to the shop before closing time and purchased exactly the right amount for dinner and furthermore if the same thing has already happened three times that month even the most devoted animal lover might be excused the fleeting desire to kick my cat.

A third problem occurs with rather depressing regularity in neutered cats. They tend, particularly in the summer, to be more prone to all sorts of skin problems than their entire brothers or sisters.

Admittedly many of these eczemas are triggered off by fleas or some other creepie-crawlie and a lot of them are further complicated by the fact that the cat has managed to bully its owner into giving it a diet consisting of one single item. Fish, for example, often turns out to be the sole diet of many cats suffering with chronic skin disorders. Nevertheless, the fact remains that the neuter is more prone to these troubles than his brother who is blessed with a full flow of male hormone.

Fortunately there are many products on the market with which one can partially replace the missing hormones. They come in all sorts of forms – pills, powder, short-acting injections, and long-acting injections. There are pellets in oil or wax which are inserted under the skin and release a steady flow of hormones for six months or longer. The formulae vary widely. Some are entirely male. Some contain a bit of female hormone. Some are synthetic. Some are natural. Some cost a few pence for several dozen. Others cost several pounds for a single injection. For some reason, best known to themselves, the Dutch and the Swiss seem to have the leading reputations in the field.

By trial and error the veterinarian tries to find the drug that just suits the particular problem. He tries to cure the condition without changing the neuter back into a tom. Of course no matter how many hormones you cram into him he will never be capable of making spermatozoa, nor will a kitten that was neutered before puberty attempt intercourse. He might, however, develop some of the other less desirable traits of the tom, like overt aggressiveness towards other males and spraying. The trick is to get the creature into a healthy balance.

The Neutered Male

There is one sort of male cat which poses a special problem. These are the cats in which either one testicle or both testicles fail to descend into the scrotal sac.

Usually the owner doesn't suspect that there is anything wrong with his kitten . . . and of course to all intents and purposes there is not. Quite often the condition is only noticed when the kitten is taken along to the veterinarian's for its neutering operation. And, in fact, every veterinarian has had the experience of being on the point of making an incision into the scrotum before realizing that in fact one or both testicles have failed to descend.

An affected cat grows into a tom with all the male characteristics of his normal brother. Although they may be sterile they compete in every sexual race that is open to the general public, and when they spray the stench that arises is indistinguishable from that produced by the tom blessed externally.

There are two much more serious disadvantages. The first is that many cats with internal testicles become incorrigibly vicious. I don't know if anyone has ever explained exactly why this should be but the same thing happens in horses. Some of the most notorious outlaws known in the rodeo world have this condition.

Second, the internal testicle becomes cancerous in an unduly high percentage of cases.

When one realizes further that this unhappy condition is hereditary one simply must agree that affected cats should be castrated. Obviously the operation is more complicated because it involves a search of the abdominal cavity. The testicle may lie anywhere from the kidney to the bladder. That distance may be only six inches or less as the ruler measures, but as the hand searches it becomes acres. It is astonishing but true that the testicle, which usually is at least as large as a pea, manages to get lost among those mountains and valleys of tissues. I have watched experienced, normally calm and placid veterinarians fulminate in helpless rage as a half hour's search stretched into an hour without success. I have heard some experienced people say that the percentage of internal testicles that are never found may be as high as twenty-five, and I believe that they are right. Sometimes after an unsuccessful operation the veterinarian will suggest that the cat be placed on a permanent course of female hormone in order to counteract the effect of the hidden testicle. This treatment often works.

Incidentally, it is an accepted rule throughout the animal-breeding world (and that includes everything from Pekinese to Percherons) not to accept for registration or for breeding any stud in which both testicles are not fully descended. When you remember that these unfortunate animals suffer more than their fair share of nervous and physical disorders and that furthermore the condition is considered hereditary, you must accept the wisdom of the ruling.

Finally we must consider an operation that by any reckoning is a sad one. That is the neutering of a full-blown tom.

The most common reason for such an operation is that Intimidating Ian has become Fearful Fred. Fights which formally he would have won without a puff now produce an endless huff, no small damage, and shameful defeat. The poor old boy has no longer got what it takes. Although he keeps trying to recapture the glories of his youth the struggle becomes increasingly difficult as season succeeds season. If you have a pet tom that has to be taken to the veterinarian three or four times in each breeding season in order to have his wounds sutured, his abscesses lanced, and his lacerations cleansed you must seriously consider whether you are doing him a favour by allowing him to retain his masculinity.

There is another reason for castrating adult toms that is all too familiar to animal welfare workers. In those wastelands which man creates each time he tears down some old buildings in order to put up new ones are to be found an assortment of cats. These descendants of domesticated cats must be captured or trapped by exactly the same methods one would use when dealing with animals of the wild. And let no one tell you that they can't be extremely dangerous!

In many places these cats are simply eliminated. They are shot, poisoned, or gassed.

Sometimes a few are rescued. A delicate, extremely feminine model I know, who one would have thought incapable of coping with a full-grown mouse, has trapped several dozens of such strays, managed to redomesticate them, and placed them in homes. Not only is it a dangerous business, but it can be very expensive as well. Almost all of that girl's very high income goes to feed and care for her strays. Sometimes it can take as long as a year or more before the cat is quiet enough to accept an ordinary home. Some cats' distrust of humans is so entrenched that they never learn to refrain from scratching at the hand that's trying to help them. In those cases one has to choose among three courses – the cat must be put to sleep, permanently caged, or released in a new area which one hopes will prove suitable.

The point is that it is universally recognized by animal welfare workers that the first step in the rehabilitation of a stray is neutering. Not only is it difficult and smelly to keep an assortment of full toms but they tend to upset all the other cats in the establishment. And, of course, they are much more difficult to place in homes than neuters.

Finally one may, for reasons either sentimental or financial, be obliged to adopt an adult tom. If your great grandmother has finally departed this good earth you may be inclined to adopt her smelly old tom as a constant reminder. If her will states that you get a million pounds provided you look after her cat you may feel a certain urgency about the inclination. If, when he moves in, one soon discovers that a choice is going to have to be made as to whether to amputate your nose or the cat's testicles, one may reasonably expect even the least vain of men to make an appointment with the veterinarian.

The preparation and the initial stages of the operation are the same for the adult as for the kitten. As the blood supply to the testicle is much greater in the adult, the veterinarian adopts one of several methods to control the haemorrhage. Some draw the vessels and cords as far out as possible and wrap a knot around them as high up as possible using any sort of material that will dissolve in the body and disappear. Others, using a couple of pairs of forceps, knot the cord and blood vessels on themselves. Still others claim that clamping the vessels with a good pair of forceps and twisting them is the simplest and best way of doing it. All agree that, as in the case of the younger kitten, suturing the scrotum is not necessary and in fact may be definitely harmful.

Naturally, as larger organs are being removed, you can expect the recuperation from the operation in the adult to take several days. It may be a fortnight or even three weeks before the old boy is back to normal. Throughout this period it is imperative that he be confined. Otherwise, in his weakened state, he will prove easy prey to his enemies.

I have seen some full toms that never appeared to regain any semblance of their former buoyancy after the operation. I am convinced that in many of those cases (although the original violation was physical) it is the psychological wound that proves permanent.

In other cases the operation seems to have no effect whatever. If the tom sprayed before the operation he continues to spray after it. And, surprisingly, some will carry on attending sexual forays as before. Some may even successfully copulate. The mating, however, would be sterile.

Most commonly, clients phone a week or so after an adult castration to complain that their cat still stinks. I reassure them that it may take another week or two before the smell entirely disappears. As these people don't phone back again we must assume that either the cat in fact does smell prettier or that the people have become immune.

It's a bit like an ageing spouse. One doesn't necessarily admire the dandruff and the falling hair, the clicking false teeth, and the assorted odours. One simply gets used to them.

3 The Entire Queen

If cats would only read the textbooks they'd realize that they're meant to deliver one or at the most two litters a year. Instead they make up their own rules as they go along.

We all know of cats that have had three litters in a year and although Nature tries to tell them not to get pregnant while nursing a litter many cats refuse to listen. Hence four litters in a year is not unknown. As the kittens must be weaned much too early they suffer in the process.

Female cats are seasonally polyoestrus. That means that given the right weather they will have several heat periods. If they are mated and become pregnant these periods stop.

The heat periods last three or four days if there is a male available and ten days or even longer if there isn't. The female usually accepts a male most readily during the last day or two of her heat. There is a two- or three-week period of comparative calm between heats.

The number of heats and the time of year in which they occur depends on both the climate and on the make-up of the individual cat.

Orientals make a mockery of everything. To their distracted

owners they appear to be always either pregnant, nursing, or calling. This is partly because they do come on heat without much regard for the calendar, and partly because when they are on heat no one within cannon range can ignore it.

It's only partly the fault of the cats that it all sounds confusing. It's also the fault of the literature available to us. Most of what we read is like the blind men's description of the elephant; each describes a different part. In the cat world some experts talk a great deal of sense about large colonies of Orientals. These cats are usually bred by people who are utterly devoted to them. The best are shown and kept for breeding, the rest are sold as pets. Other descriptions are of ordinary cats in laboratories. Few concern themselves with ordinary cats living ordinary lives. And you can be sure that when anyone writes long articles about his 'ordinary' cat, the cat turns out to be quite special.

One authority states that the periods of heat in Northern Europe are in the spring and early autumn. Another states that in Algiers they're mid-December to the end of January and mid-July to the end of August, but some females may be found in heat from January to July. Another says that in the northern United States few cats are in heat between September and January.

One report on two hundred female cats in an English laboratory states that most of the cats came on season many times during January and February, then again (but not so many times) in June and July. The average duration of heat was three days and the interval between heats about ten days. The average period of pregnancy was sixty-one to sixty-three days and the average size of a litter was four.

May I make a longwinded comment? I was once a part owner of a large piggery. We had a hundred sows in a long narrow building. We had a dozen in scattered outbuildings. In the large building each time one sow lay down and the piglets came pushing and grunting for their suckle all the other piglets in the place started grunting. And all the poor old sows, even those that were enjoying a well-earned sleep, were forced to respond. In the outbuildings where sows and their young were housed singly, each family kept to their own individual rhythm. Is it too far-fetched to suggest that cats in large catteries trigger each other sexually in a similar manner? Would the pattern be so nice and neat if they were kept individually? How about those that are not kept at all? Do they act the same? I wish I knew.

Let's start with puberty. This is the period when the kitten starts to become a cat. The dictionary tells us it's the age when an animal is functionally capable of procreation. Many texts put the age of puberty for the cat at about fifteen months. I don't know how they came to that figure. In my experience a queen is usually well started on her second litter by that age.

What does the owner see? His playful kitten of five or six or eight months becomes far more affectionate. She will not merely accept affection or occasionally suggest that it's time for a bit of reciprocal tenderness. She'll demand it. She'll rub herself incessantly against legs both human and table. If a kind hand strokes her she'll crouch and raise her tail. She may roll ecstatically. She may quiver exotically. She may convulse rhythmically or shiver epileptically. She can look and act quite crazy. If this sounds far-fetched ask your veterinarian how many times he's had emergency calls about kittens dying in extreme pain when in fact the kitten turns out to be experiencing nothing more than a normal heat. Ask your R.S.P.C.A. man how many complaints of neighbours torturing cats turn out to lead to a cat on heat.

And just to be perverse may I point out that some owners report they've never seen their cat on heat. There she is with a boxful of kittens and no one noticed anything out of the ordinary. There are three possible explanations. The first is that the owners are unobservant. Some people wouldn't notice if their spouse sprouted wings. The second is that some cats may be undemonstrative in the same way that some people are. The third is that the creature reserves her display for those able to fulfil her requirements.

A spoiled, home-loving kitten probably won't brave the

great unknown world beyond her garden during her first heat. In fact if a tom or any other cat comes towards her she'll rush indoors to her trusted human protector. There, without conscious will, she'll resume her seductive rolls and rubs and frustrated cries and calls. She'll wonder why they don't know what she wants. Meanwhile the toms will take note. Frightening apparitions they may be to her the first time around, but their time will come. A bit later, usually about a fortnight, the kitten will go through it again. It may take two or three more such sessions before the kitten's urgent needs overcome her reluctance to leave home and humans to temporarily rejoin her kind.

Some particularly doting (or is it dotty?) owners think that they can keep their cat both entire and entirely to themselves.

They say they can't cope with kittens and yet they believe neutering or doctoring of cats to be unnatural, cruel, and destructive of the cat's real personality. They keep the poor creature locked up during her seasons. This is perfectly all right when she is a kitten. She'll soon forget those few weeks of frustration, and it's better if she's allowed to go an extra few months before becoming a mother. But if this forcible restraint is continued into adulthood it must produce a frustrated, neurotic creature. Everything in her nature must say go and the closed door says no. I once knew a Siamese queen that had been locked up like that for eight years. She must have suffered considerably through her scores of heat periods. Her owner, as neurotic a crone as you're likely to meet, swore that she loved the cat more than life itself and insisted that the cat was such a dependent creature that bearing kittens would overwhelm her delicate balance. Nor could Petunia survive 'the agony of an operation'. As it happened, pregnancy almost killed that cat. After eight years of frustration she found her way to freedom and a tom. The first the owner knew about it was when the poor creature went into labour. I suppose one could compare the cat's ordeal with that of a sixty-year-old woman bearing her first child. She couldn't bear them naturally. An operation was performed. All the kittens were dead. The veterinarian in charge wisely decided to remove her uterus and ovaries at the same time so that the poor animal wouldn't have to go through it again. The point of this story is that female cats, no matter how old, have an overwhelming drive to reproduce. You should allow them to do so or have them doctored. Locking them up is cruel.

What about kittens that are not dependent on human affection and protection? These include the majority of farm and warehouse cats, all strays and semi-wild cats, and the minority of cats owned by families who believe that their sole responsibility is a saucer of milk whenever someone is sober enough to remember. Puberty for these kittens no matter how small, young, or under-developed almost always means pregnancy. At their first heat they're bred. Even if they wanted to they couldn't avoid the platoons of waiting toms. Among these semiferal cats one often sees a litter of kittens suckling a mother that is nothing but a kitten herself.

Their fortunate cousins include the majority of pure-bred cats. These, despite their beauty, their pedigrees, and their well-merited coddling, come on heat without a blush. Siamese, Burmese, Abyssinians, and other Orientals too are the same as other cats except more so. Most put on a display that would put a Beirut belly dancer to shame.

The actual physical act of union is roughly the same for all cats regardless of breed or climate. Most (if they have an escape route back to the security of their home) will not accept males until they are ready. And a cat is not ready for mating until its ovary is 'ripe' with eggs. These eggs or ova are not released until after copulation. There is a great deal of evidence that the cat is one of the few species of animal that actually requires the stimulation of copulation before ovulation takes place. But more of that a bit later.

The female on heat may give a characteristic cry, called 'calling'. Although the male may respond to that call the prime sexual magnet is the scent of the female on heat.

As the male approaches, the queen, depending upon her stage of receptivity, may continue to call; she may tread, roll, and generally ingratiate herself, or she may run away, or she may in typical perverse female unpredictability turn on the tom in apparent fury. Experienced toms bide their time. Others, less experienced or more eager, may circle closer. Under natural conditions, there may be a small in-circle of toms who, oblivious to the hisses of the female, press on with their courtship while outside other toms avoid boredom by hissing at each other. Removed even further from the fray there may be one or two wise old boys conserving their energies for later. They'll make a start when the hissing comes to a stop.

When the female is almost ready she rolls in front of the male. She may rub her nose and mouth against objects, she may call continuously, she may crouch, and she may tread with her feet. However, more than a few have been known to strike out at the male even at that late stage. Finally, however, even a queen from the best of homes will allow the male to approach.

As the male grips the skin of her neck firmly with his teeth the female elevates her hindquarters and bends in such a way that her vulva is facing almost straight upwards. At the same time she treads with her hind legs and whips her tail to the side so that her orifice is exposed.

As the male inserts his penis the female gives a characteristic cry. Some people say it's a howl of pain; others feel it's rage. I don't know why we can't relax our puritanical code and hope that it's pleasure.

One explanation given by people who believe that the cat's characteristic copulatory cry is one of pain is the fact that the tomcat's penis is covered with hard barbs. They think that such a raspy organ must cause pain. They postulate that the cry we hear occurs when the penis is forcibly withdrawn against the lie of the barbs.

Well, let me describe an experiment which was done over thirty years ago in California. Using a smooth glass rod about the same diameter as a cat's penis, and tapering to a rounded point as does the penis, a scientist evinced the typical behaviour and cry of a cat experiencing natural intercourse. He noted that pressing the rod upward, downward, or to either side did not produce any marked response. It was only when the rod was pressed straight forward towards the cervix that the cat gave the typical cry. Please note that (a) the rod was smooth and (b) the cry was given on insertion, not withdrawal.

The man who did this really wasn't concerned whether cats experienced pleasure, or orgasm for that matter. He was setting out to prove that neither natural intercourse nor male spermatozoa were necessary to stimulate ovulating in the cat. In nine out of his twelve subjects stimulation with the glass rod was followed by ovulation, so he did prove his point. His work also suggested that if the ovary isn't ripe to drop its eggs no sort of stimulation will induce it to do so. In other words, even though the cat is on heat her ovary may not be quite ready and mating doesn't work. She needs the ripe ovary plus the stimulus of intercourse.

In the majority of cases the cat is receptive only when the ovary is ripe, so one can say that her nature follows the dictates of both economics and common sense. In the ferret too copulation is thought to be a necessary stimulus for ovulation. In most other species of animal ovulation occurs quite independently. The eggs ripen and drop at rhythmic intervals. If the male mounts the female successfully at the right time the eggs unite with the sperm and a new life begins. If there is no male about the eggs are wasted.

The scientist who manipulated the glass rod described how the cats behaved after its withdrawal. He said they 'rolled from side to side – almost frantically, in some cases. The periods of rolling were interrupted by intervals which the animal devoted to licking the vulva and to rubbing itself vigorously, especially its head and back, against any suitable, available object. This period of activity was followed by one during which the animal lay quietly on its side, often purring softly and "opening and closing" its front paws – behaviour which is usually interpreted as indicative of a feeling of contentment and well-being. If the animal had only just come on heat, or if it had been stimulated only once or twice, it would ordinarily submit willingly to a repetition of the procedure within fifteen minutes to a half hour after the beginning of the inactive phase just described.'*

He went on to say that he watched cats having natural coitus and the behaviour differed in no essential detail.

Twenty-seven years later, in 1961, another scientist named Michael published a summary of his observations on hundreds of cats.† Over a period of five years he had conducted several thousand mating tests. He divides the sexual cycle into four phrases and although they may appear at first reading to be slightly complicated a careful study will reveal that in fact it's a very simple system. Once you grasp the idea it's much easier to understand the behaviour of any particular female cat.

The first phase is called anoestrous. During this phase the queen is simply not interested in any sexual advances which the male may care to make. Should the tom approach her too closely she will spit and strike at him. If he gets close enough to sniff her vulva he immediately turns away. Otherwise the full tom and the anoestrous female appear completely indifferent to each other.

The second stage is called pro-oestrous. This is the stage between indifference to or complete rejection of the tom as occurs in anoestrous and the stage of true heat in which mating occurs.

The female in pro-oestrous moves about her pen rubbing her flanks along the wall. Later on that day or the day following she starts to rub herself against every object. At this stage we would say that she appears very affectionate. She rubs almost continuously against anything with her head and neck.

If the tom approaches she is not nearly so hostile. During the next twenty-four hours she rubs even more and she starts rolling. She also purrs and squirms and stretches, and opens and closes her claws rhythmically. During this stage the male's interest, not surprisingly, increases. The queen will let him

* Greulich, William Walter, 'Artificially Induced Ovulation in the Cat (Felis Domestica),' Anatomical Record, Vol. 58, No. 3, February, 1934.

† Michael, Richard P., 'Observations Upon the Sexual Behaviour of the Domestic Cat (Felis catus 1.) Under Laboratory Conditions,' *Behaviour* 1961, Vol. 18.

approach and lick her head and vulva. He watches her as she rolls and as she moves about rubbing her head against the walls he follows her. He will try when the opportunity presents itself to grab her neck preparatory to mounting. At this stage, however, she is still not ready, and refuses him by hissing, spitting, and clawing. As he jumps clear she again begins to roll. Then she squirms on her belly towards him. If he attempts to mount her again she rebuffs him. At this stage the older male still bides his time while the younger, over-eager tom may attempt to mount and get bitten. Sometimes the queen partly crouches; sometimes she treads. Towards the end of pro-oestrous she starts to call softly.

Pro-oestrous may last only twenty-four hours before the queen accepts the male. Other queens may carry on that stage for three days before they become receptive to the tom. The scientist noted that each individual queen was remarkably constant in the length of that period.

The third stage is called oestrous. This is the period of true heat or complete sexual receptivity. The female changes dramatically. During pro-oestrous she aggressively refused the tom. During oestrous she accepts him completely.

The first signal of the onset of oestrous is that given when the female interrupts her rolling and squirming and assumes the mating posture. The male immediately mounts and grips her neck. Michael notes that this change may occur so rapidly that an inexperienced observer might miss it. The queen crouches with her body right against the floor. She lifts her rear, holds her tail to one side, and begins to tread with her hind limbs. She treads more quickly as the male thrusts. During one of those movements the tom inserts his penis. As he does so the queen cries, jumps free, and spits and scratches. Meanwhile, the male jumps clear. The total time involved from neck grip to finish is about four minutes. The actual insertion of the penis and its withdrawal takes from five to fifteen seconds.

The queen then licks her vulva and begins to roll violently in what is called the after reaction. The male stays a few feet away. The queen's rolling gradually subsides, and about half an hour later she accepts the male for the second time. In that particular laboratory and that particular series of observations some queens accepted the tom only eleven minutes after the previous consummation. Other queens weren't receptive for an hour and a half. These intervals increased during the ensuing hours. Some couples kept going for twenty-four hours – others for forty-eight.

The fourth and final stage is called metoestrous. This is the tapering-off period which occurs after true oestrous. It may last as long as twenty-four hours. During metoestrous the female will allow the male to mount but she will not allow him to insert his penis. As he thrusts and she treads preparatory to insertion she suddenly bursts into anger and turns on him.

At the end of metoestrous the queen returns to anoestrous. She rejects all the tom's advances as if she'd never known that gentleman. If he approaches her she lashes out in a paroxysm of fury. If, however, he is content to mind his own business she is quite happy to ignore his presence.

Michael proved beyond dispute that those four stages do in fact exist. He showed that for each stage of sexual behaviour there was a corresponding change in the cells of the vagina which could be demonstrated under the microscope. One *can* question the actual times of the various activities and the intervals between them, because aside from the fact that each laboratory must impose its own conditions on the cats, every group of cats, however selected, is composed of individuals. And anyone who has lived with cats, can bear witness to the wide variations possible between individuals.

There are two other observations from that report which are extremely interesting. Although they concern the behaviour of the stud cat, I include them here for convenience. The first is that although the toms were selected from among a group of healthy and mature cats only one in three became 'really reliable and vigorous test animals'.

The second observation bears out the experience of many breeders of pure-breds. It concerns the fact that tomcats in captivity perform more vigorously if they are in familiar home territory. If, however, the stud cat is a well-loved pet he will perform anywhere provided his human owner is standing by. As Michael put it, 'the presence of the familiar human being appears in some way to have the effect of conferring territory-right'.*

There must be many variations on this sexual theme outside the walls of a laboratory or the confines of a cattery. During the breeding season every veterinarian in small-animal practice sees an assortment of battle-scarred toms that would gratify the most bloodthirsty Hollywood producer. And towards the end of a breeding season all the toms that live a semi-natural existence are gaunt beyond belief, obviously bored with the company of their own kind, and grateful for human care and companionship. When one compares those toms to the ones that have been meeting females in cages one realizes that the circle of competing and fighting cats must add a ringside excitement and pressure to the game.

If the female has been successfully mated she usually becomes pregnant. Outwardly she appears unchanged. She resumes her normal habits. Inwardly her body changes as it undertakes its most important task – the production of new life.

* *Op. cit.*

4 The Neutered Female

TO SPAY OR NOT TO SPAY

My doctor is a mad Irishman who stutters. He has been my doctor so many years that his youngest daughter whom I used to tease now teases me. His practice is a large chaotic amorphous affair in which somehow every single patient feels that he really matters. The reason they feel that way is that they do. Where his patients are concerned no trouble is too much; no hour inconvenient. In return, as you might expect, the patients have no small regard for their doctor. This regard embraces (I use that verb in its most innocent sense) his charming wife. In any large general practice the wife does everything short of actually signing the prescriptions.

An autobiographical urge is not my reason for giving you these background facts. I am just trying to say that my doctor's wife knows an awful lot of people. Also, to say that she likes cats is an understatement. She dotes on them. A few years back she acquired a female kitten; quite an ordinary, black, catlike kitten.

When the kitten was about eight months of age she proudly presented a litter of five kittens. These she raised easily, weaned naturally, and appeared not to miss at all when they went to their new homes.

Four and a half months after the birth of her first litter there came another. There were six. Again, there were no problems.

And so it went for some years. She appeared quite happy having her average of two and a half litters per year. Or at least one may infer that she was because she became terribly unhappy if any attempt was made to restrict her breeding activity. In all, she produced one hundred and twenty kittens before we decided (after repeated consultations) to have her spayed.

Why did we make this decision? The cat was apparently quite willing and able to go on indefinitely. The good doctor's wife, however, was not. She had run out of friends, clients, and acquaintances who would offer a kitten a good home.

No matter how she cajoled, the placing of kittens became more and more difficult. Some people already had a cat and didn't want another. Some people possessed packs of terriers and thought it would be unfair to introduce a young kitten to them. Other people lived beside roads officially known as 'Death Alley' and informally referred to as 'Bloody Lane'.

Some people were heartbroken because they couldn't have a kitten. They explained that for many years their family had had dozens of cats. They had also had a persistent itch which couldn't be controlled even during solemn church services or in the intervals of expensive operas. Only when their psychiatrists told them to get rid of the cats did the light dawn. A surprising number responded that they had spent so long in the Far East that they could hardly guarantee to refrain from cooking the creatures and eating them. And a few confessed that apart from snakes their greatest fear was that a cat would eat them.

All in all, as the years went by it became increasingly difficult to place the kittens. The point of this whole chapter is that if my dear doctor's dedicated wife (with all her persuasiveness and contacts) could only find homes for one hundred and twenty kittens how many kittens do you think you can place?

Surely, many people say, with all the advances of medical science and all the marvellous fences available on the market it must be possible to restrict a queen's production to a more sensible three or four litters during her lifetime.

Let's first take a look at the fences. The female cat on heat is not noted for her subtlety. She was put on this earth to test the cage makers. And even if the barriers you put up prove successful your ears may not be able to withstand the resulting din. After a few sleepless nights most owners surrender. They recall reading somewhere that the unmated queen stays on heat several days longer than those that are allowed access to a tom.

Some people have the facilities in which to lock a queen well out of earshot each and every time she comes on season. Other people are deaf. They enforce a celibate existence on a creature whose every instinct is directed to reproducing itself. Inevitably the cat suffers. Sometimes it's her uterus which becomes infected. It becomes swollen and painful and the cat becomes thin and apathetic. Sometimes, in more acute cases, the cat suddenly begins to drink enormous quantities of water, goes off her food completely, or vomits whatever she does eat. In either case the remedy is surgical. The uterus and ovaries must be removed.

Sometimes the cat's body can cope with its unnatural deprivation but its mind cannot. Some of them get a fixation about courtship. This phase of the sexual act normally lasts from a few seconds to as long as five minutes. In the frustrated female it may continue for hour after endless hour. She crouches. She rolls over and over. She paddles with her legs non-stop as if she were on an endless treadmill. She rubs her face against objects, sometimes until it is sore and bleeding. And she cries!

Other deprived females of mature years have been seen to go through the complete motions of copulation for long periods. The female cat during normal copulation bends her tail to one side and swings her hind end to accommodate the male for a period of about ten seconds. The cat going through an imaginary act may hold this position for as long as half an hour.

Still others endlessly pretend that they have just been served. They lick their paws and their external sexual organs furiously. These post-copulatory activities usually last less than five minutes if the female has in fact been mounted by a tom. In the isolated female they may last for hours.

Some people say that all of these activities are in fact those of the female cat experiencing a normal heat. Admittedly there is some overlap. I hope that I am being neither too sentimental, anthropomorphic, nor subjective when I say that to me there is a distinct difference between the activities of the frustrated female and those of the normal cat in heat. The one is neurotic if not demented. The other is optimistic anticipation.

One does not expect a cat to go loony just because she's been locked up during one or two heat periods. It is those that are deprived of a male year after year that are most likely to cross that border.

Still other deprived females become nervous, anxious, easily frightened, and apparently at ease only when they are hiding in some inaccessible corner. Some breeders who keep as many as half a dozen or a dozen queens find that it pays them handsomely in terms of peace and quiet if they keep a vasectomized tomcat. These are tomcats that have had a minor operation which renders them sterile but in all other respects they remain normal toms. Veterinarians usually suggest that the operation be done when a tom is six or seven months of age. When he becomes a year or a year and a half of age he will mate the less aggressive queens, and later he will be able to cope with the lot. Although the queens don't become pregnant they are apparently satisfied psychologically by the procedure and quieten down as if they were. Later if one wishes to mate the queen with a normal tom one isolates her for two or three weeks. When she cycles back into a normal heat she may be mated.

What about The Pill? As I understand it, it is mainly composed of a hormone which says to the body, 'You are now pregnant. You therefore do not need to bother any longer.'

Aside from the moral aspects there seems to be a continuing debate about their use in human beings. One widely spread conclusion is that those which are the safest and have the fewest side effects are the least effective.

There are several preparations based on the same hormone (progesterone) which are used to prevent mating, pregnancy, or both in the dog. One which was used on both sides of the Atlantic for several years was an injection which prevented the female dog from coming on season for a period of about six months. It was also used to a limited extent in cats. At first it was used without a great deal of discrimination. Then it was pointed out that some dogs and some cats, including greyhounds and Siamese, were not suited to the drug. Later it was pointed out that only in exceptional circumstances should the injection be given before the animal had had at least one normal season. Later still veterinarians were warned to assess the dosage much more carefully than they had been used to doing.

Then reports came in from many different practising veterinarians. A disquieting number of animals were developing infected wombs as well as other ailments that were rendering them useless for breeding purposes. And inevitably there were a few losses. Finally the drug was withdrawn from the market.

Lately with a great deal of fanfare two companies have introduced similar products to Britain. These too are forms of progesterone.

One form, which comes in tablets only, is not recommended for cats. The other, which comes in both tablet and injectable form, may be used, according to the drug company, on cats. And I have no doubt that it will be widely used for at least a year or two. The veterinarian may be slightly doubtful about it but even he (appearances notwithstanding) is human. On the one hand he is subjected to pressures which only clients know how to apply and on the other hand he is reassured by a travelling representative that he is the only veterinarian for many miles around who has the slightest doubts about the safety of the product.

Why do the clients bring this pressure to bear? Why, even after they are told that we have yet to discover the drug which can safely suppress oestrus in the cat and that there is a distinct possibility that a few days or weeks after the injection the cat will come down with an infected uterus and have to have it removed, do they still insist that something be done?

Owners of Siamese are particularly insistent because their cats are particularly vocal. And when you remember that the female on heat calls for four days if she is allowed a tom but prolongs the screams a further six if she is not, you may have a certain sympathy.

When you further consider that the human assistance and extra cleaning involved in rearing a litter of kittens can sometimes almost constitute a full-time job it is no marvel that quite normal people refuse to go through it more than once a year.

'Let her occupy herself with the commendable female activities like being mounted, being pregnant, undergoing labour, and nursing a litter for one half of the year. I am more than willing to help. But surely,' they implore, 'it's not too much to ask that for the other half of the year she gives herself and us a rest?'

Why, you might sensibly ask, do these people not have their cats operated on and eliminate the problem once and for all? There are many reasons – some of them valid.

Some people have two or three very good pure-bred queens and they enjoy mating them and they enjoy even more the income from the sale of kittens. They're not avaricious or even commercial. They like having a hobby which partly pays for itself. On the other hand they don't wish to get involved in a full-time activity.

Some of us like to plan our holidays, marriages, divorces, and other events well in advance. And it is rather a bore to arrive at the desert island of your choice only to be handed a telegram saying you must return at once because Charlotte is pregnant. Sometimes one's travelling companion, despite all the earnest explanations, simply will not accept that Charlotte is a cat.

A great many people want their queen to have a 'normal' life but they don't want her to drain herself in the process. They feel that she should have at least a six-month's rest between litters, and I must agree that it seems a good idea in theory. In practice, however, the six months of frustration seem to cause more illness (both physical and mental) than the continual production of kittens.

Other people (like those who refuse to have their male cats castrated) feel that the operation is heartless, cruel, and unnatural. It is certainly unnatural. We may hope that some day a drug will be perfected that will allow the female cat both to remain herself and at the same time remain a pleasure rather than a drain to her human owners. At the moment of writing no such product is in the offing.

Those who are opposed to the neutering of female cats must first accept that unhappy fact and secondly recognize that throughout much of the world there are too many cats. Animals, when left to their own devices, regulate the growth of their populations. Only when man interferes does one get a shortage or even the disappearance in some species and an embarrassing surplus in others. Even behind the Iron Curtain, where from time to time campaigns are held to eradicate useless bourgeois pets, a surplus exists in most years. My evidence for this is that there is a thriving trade from eastern Europe in the hides of these cats. Thousands upon thousands are slaughtered and skinned each year. Before you rush into a hasty condemnation of the Reds let me remind you that the demand for 'fun-furs' in the West is apparently insatiable.

If a surplus of cats exists in a country where they are trapped and hunted, how much greater is the problem in countries where both practices are frowned upon? And, in the main, the lot of the stray is an unhappy one. The struggle for survival is often harsh. Most stray kittens soon learn about cold and hunger. They learn about competition as soon as they take their first faltering steps out of the nest. Some experienced animal welfare workers estimate that less than 50 per cent of kittens born to strays reach six months of age.

Those that do survive the harsh system are usually agile, tough, and intelligent enough to carve themselves out a fairly decent niche for the first few years. But they are subject to every hazard of climate, disease, and traffic. What would represent only a slight inconvenience to the pet cat might be the beginning of the end for a stray.

When they reach middle age a short period of deprivation or illness precipitates them rapidly into old age and death. Anyone who has ever seen a cadaverous old queen with a broken pelvis trying to cross a busy main road in order to reach her suckling kittens must think twice before adding a single stray to the cat population.

Another strong argument for neutering female cats is that provided by people who casually acquire a kitten, and when it in turn produces kittens equally casually discard them. On countless occasions I have been presented with a boxful of little lives by a child. 'Daddy says to put them to sleep, we got too many already.'

Sometimes I find the box of kittens on the doorstep. Sometimes they are stuffed into a shopping bag and on one occasion quite a larger ginger – I reckoned him to be about ten weeks old – was pushed through my letter box.

What about the actual operation? When should it be done? What does it involve? Is there any age limit? What care is needed at home after the operation? And what are the after effects of the operation? Will she be changed?

Most people agree that it's a good idea to have a cat spayed before she becomes pregnant. The onset of the first heat varies a bit, according to the time of year and the type of cat. Although even the most authoritative textbooks still persist in stating that this first season occurs between six and eight months of age, in practice we find that many kittens become pregnant at five months.

Many veterinarians advise people to allow their kitten to have her first heat but to keep her away from toms. This is not too difficult for one occasion and as the first heat is rather a short one even those people with the most expensive psychiatrists can usually put up with it. A week or so later, book her in for the operation.

Some people think it doesn't matter if the kitten is a week or two or even three weeks pregnant when she has her ovario-hysterectomy. They say that it's the best of all possible compromises. The kitten has reached a certain maturity with the full benefit of her female hormones. This I must agree is true. They also say that she has had the experience of being successfully mated and this too must confer a certain maturity. Most scientists say this is a rather sentimental approach, based on human experience and without any validity in the animal world. As far as the actual surgery involved is concerned there is not a great deal of difference. Statistics from veterinary hospitals would no doubt show that the mortality rates of cats spayed before they are mated and those when they are two or three weeks' pregnant would be about the same.

A considerable number of people feel that the female kitten should be allowed to mature and produce one litter, and for many many people and for many many cats this is, I agree, an ideal compromise. The cat has the benefit of growing into true maturity. She grows into adulthood while receiving her full quota of hormones – even those that have yet to be discovered. And, as is the case with some women, the bearing of young which must include labour, nursing, and weaning confers other benefits as well. We all know women who are self-centred, nervous, or even neurotic, completely selfish and inconsiderate of the needs or feelings of others, until the birth of their first child. For some, as we sadly know, it is the beginning of the end. They simply cannot cope. That child represents an affirmation of adult responsibility which they realize with a dreadful finality they do not want. The psychiatrists who have to cope with that kind of tragedy have my full sympathy.

For the majority of people, however, and for almost every female cat, the bearing of young is a liberation. The busy responsibilities of motherhood leave them no time for the tiny fears of yesterday and when they have finished controlling and teaching their young they themselves have learned how to more effectively control their own fears and their own aggression.

I am not suggesting that all female cats would benefit by having a litter. Many are stable and delightful as kittens and remain that way whether they have kittens or whether they are neutered. Then there are cats that are so crazy as kittens that one would hesitate to breed them. First, one would hate to take a chance on making them slightly crazier. Some kittens that appear to be walking a thin line between a kind of normality and an outright scattiness are definitely helped by the neutering operation. After the removal of the ovaries they seem to be able to live a much quieter existence. Second, any serious-thinking person would not wish to help bring into the world a litter of kittens that have every likelihood of resembling their crazy mother. That is, of course, if one suspects that the condition is hereditary. Every professional cat breeder can name several strains of purebred cats (not one of which they've ever had anything to do with, thank goodness) that have been recognizably nutty for as many generations as they have been recognized as purebreds. They have clawed and spat at the show judges for so many years that those poor souls have learned to hang the championship ribbons on the outside of the cages and hurry on to the next section. If you have been sold one of these handsome candidates for a strait jacket, please ignore all the blandishments of the breeder and have her spayed.

Quite often cats become incorrigibly vicious following an injury to the brain. They can manage to eat and clean themselves and walk about without losing their balance, but if anyone at all attempts to handle them they fly into a paroxysm of fury. Some people, for reasons best known to themselves, refuse to have such a cat put down. They should, however, seriously consider having her spayed. The strongest argument one can put forward is that she is quite likely to do a great deal of damage to the tom during mating; and she is even more likely to turn on her own kittens and kill them.

THE OPERATION AND ITS EFFECTS

Anaesthetizing the female cat for her operation is no different than doing the male for his. Naturally, as the operation on the female is a more complicated one and is likely to take longer, she must get a bit more.

First the hair over the site of the operation is clipped off, and the skin is thoroughly cleaned and disinfected. This is done by a nurse while the surgeon scrubs with the same diligence as you hope your own doctor used when he yanked out your appendix.

Many veterinarians prefer to make their initial incision exactly along the mid-line of the abdomen. It runs from just around the navel back about half an inch or an inch. That seems to be the most popular site used by American veterinarians. They say it's a nice accessible area, easily clipped and cleaned, and once they're in the abdomen they can easily pick up the uterus and trace it back to the ovary on each side.

In Britain and in Australasia many veterinarians prefer to make their incision on the flank. The site is about half an inch below the spine just in front of the point of the hip. Although it requires a bit more effort to clean the area properly and it requires a certain knack to find the uterus underneath it, the veterinarians who use this method say that its primary advantage is that almost always healing is very rapid and the danger of hernia is minimal. The one big disadvantage of this method is that in many cats, particularly Siamese and Burmese, the hair may grow back a different shade, creating a permanent patch about two or three inches square which is either lighter or darker in colour than the surrounding coat. Most owners, however, prefer to take a chance on this rather slight cosmetic defect rather than risk a hernia.

Whichever site the veterinarian uses, he cuts through the skin, the underlying connective tissues and muscles, and finally the peritoneum (which is the glistening inner protective membrane which we all have), and thus enters the abdominal cavity.

Then using either forceps or something that looks like a button hook he picks up one horn of the Y-shaped uterus.

This he easily traces back to the ovary. At the far side of the ovary he finds a blood vessel which he ties off with a tiny ligature or two. Then he snips off the ovary and that branch of the uterus and traces it back down to the other branch and its ovary, where he repeats the procedure. Then he ties a suture or two at the base of the uterus, where the two branches come together, and removes the lot.

He checks for a second to see that all is well and there is no internal haemorrhage, then joins the edges of the severed peritoneum with a stitch or two, puts another couple in the muscle layer, and adds one or two in the skin. The important stitches are those in the peritoneum. Generally if it is properly joined the cat can tear the outer layers as it wishes without doing itself any real injury.

Many experienced veterinarians can do this entire operation, from the initial incision to the final stitch, in less than five minutes. Many people on hearing this suggest that the average charge for the operation is therefore outrageous. One must point out to them that the veterinarian may have been doing it for a dozen years and only reached that stage of casual perfection after, say, half a dozen years of doing half a dozen a day. One is paying the fee precisely because the operation has been simplified and perfected.

I once saw a brilliant surgeon of international reputation attempt to spay a cat. He was a professor who had demonstrated techniques that he himself had perfected before a score of students on closed-circuit TV. His experience with humans helped him not at all, and it helped the cat even less. The poor creature had an incision over three inches long, her peritoeum wasn't properly closed after the operation, and the whole wound broke down and had to be redone by a veterinary surgeon. I am not for a moment suggesting that surgeons who practise on the human are incompetent; they've chosen their species and we've chosen ours.

Sometimes the veterinarian only finds out that the cat is pregnant after she has been anaesthetized. He almost always proceeds with the operation, because in most cases the kittens would have been killed or injured by the anaesthetic. If she's less than a month in kitten the additional risk isn't that great. Naturally the surgeon will have to spend longer, because the blood vessels to the area will all be engorged. They must enlarge to feed those growing lives. And of course the suturing must be done very carefully indeed!

Also, the incision will be much longer. The uterus at its widest point may be two inches or more and one can hardly expect to pull a mass like that through a very tiny incision.

If the cat is more than a month pregnant the uterus may be quite enormous. I have seen some removed in which each horn was about eight inches long and about three inches thick. The owners are usually quite horrified when they see the eight or ten stitches that are needed. I occasionally have to remind them that it's hardly my fault that the cat got in that condition. And of course I mollify them by pointing out that old surgical truism that wounds heal from side to side, not from end to end.

Of course there is a lot more shock following an operation of that magnitude. Sometimes the cat has to be put on an intravenous drip for some hours afterwards. Almost always the veterinarian will want to keep her in overnight or possibly a couple of extra days. And her activities will have to be seriously curtailed, for at least a fortnight.

The ordinary case (the cat that is not pregnant when she is spayed) is usually allowed to go home the day of the operation. The after care that she needs is exactly the same as that needed for her brother after his operation, described in Chapter 2, 'The Neutered Male'. The only additional complication you may occasionally expect to see in the female during the first week of convalescence is a breakdown of the stitches or an infection underneath them.

Veterinarians are always asked by their clients why they don't bandage around the abdomen of the cat, and thus protect the site of the operation. Some veterinarians do. Most, however, find that a sizeable fraction of their patients would have such bandages off within minutes of their waking. Cats (and many dogs) simply will not accept anything tightly bound around their bodies. And of course if the bandage is loose, it serves no purpose.

Most veterinarians use very fine silk or nylon for the external layer of sutures (those used to pull the skin together), and although most cats will give the area a desultory lick they soon accept them. After a week or ten days the opening is healed over and the silk or nylon stitches may be removed.

If the cat removes a single stitch or even all the external stitches there is no reason to panic, provided she doesn't expose a great gaping hole. Usually the stitches underneath will still hold while the skin heals itself. The scar will be larger, of course, but after a week or so this too will disappear.

If you see a gaping hole rather than glistening tissue where the stitches have pulled out or been pulled out then you must call the veterinarian. Some will want the cat brought in immediately. Others may be quite certain because of their technique that the inner stitches will hold, and will feel safe waiting until the next day before seeing her.

Very, very rarely, thank goodness, the cat attacks the area with a ferocity which ignores her own pain, and really opens it up. Intestines and other tissues pour out. Sometimes the owner is fortunate enough to see it shortly after it has happened. Try and round up two friends to help. Have one hold the cat by the scruff of her neck very firmly indeed, and by the hind legs as well. Have the other soak a towel in water, wring it out, and wrap it around the cat's abdomen. Meanwhile, get on the phone to the veterinarian. If he's not in keep phoning till you find one who is.

The veterinarian will anaesthetize the cat, wash the whole area with sterile salt water several times, ease the tissues back into the cavity, and sew it up. When the cat wakes up she'll find her head encased in an Elizabethan collar and her feet bandaged. Uncomfortable as it is she'll stay like that until the incision is completely healed.

Sometimes the owner discovers the damage when it's too late. The cat has not only opened up the wound but has partially chewed and clawed her own tissues. Usually the shock and damage is too much. The cat is destroyed.

May I emphasize that this is a very rare tragedy! For some years I have attended an R.S.P.C.A. emergency clinic that is located within walking distance of Piccadilly. This clinic caters to all sorts of accidents, emergencies, injured strays, frightened cats up trees, frightened dogs cowering under cars, injured swans from the Royal Parks, and on one memorable occasion a snake from Soho that had been trodden on by its owner during an energetic striptease. The responsibility is shared among a half dozen or so central London veterinarians. I, or one of my partners or assistants, am on duty every sixth week-end and every other Thursday evening. The point of this verbal detour is that although that clinic sees cases from all over London (whenever the animal's own veterinarian is not available) I can only recall seeing two such complicated cases.

A rather more common complication is a stitch abscess. The majority of these are caused, I am ashamed to say, by a slip-up in technique. Sometimes the suturing material has not been properly sterilized. Sometimes the skin has not been properly cleansed. There can be a dozen or more causes. I know of few veterinary hospitals that don't have at least one panic session every other year in which three or four patients in a row are discovered to have stitch abscesses. The place is turned upside down until the source of the trouble is discovered and put right.

How do you recognize a stitch abscess? There is a sore, tender swelling at the site of the operation. If you try to touch it the cat may lash out at you. She herself will be uncomfortable, out of sorts, and usually off her feed. The only effective home aid is gentle bathing with lukewarm water with plenty of salt in it (three of four tablespoons of salt to a pint of water). Provided you apply no pressure whatever, the cat after half a moment of resistance will appreciate your help.

You do this only to relieve her while waiting for the garage to send a man to fix the tyre on the car so that you can take her to the veterinarian's (we all know that problems never occur singly). If the infection is small and superficial the veterinarian may advise that you merely continue with the bathing. If it is deep or involves more tissue he'll almost certainly give an injection of antibiotic, drain the infection, and possibly restitch. Some become even more complicated and the patient must be hospitalized for some days or weeks.

A small percentage of cats reject the internal sutures. Catgut, which practically all veterinarians use, is meant to dissolve and be gradually absorbed, and that is what usually happens. But it is a foreign material (for despite its name it is made from the intestine of sheep) and the cat's body vigorously defends itself against foreign material. This phenomenon – which is called, obviously enough, gut rejection – often means that the whole incision will open up within a day or two or three of the operation. Usually the cat is re-admitted, anaesthetized, and resutured with cotton or silk or nylon, and everyone fevently hopes that the cat's body will not reject those materials. The reason they are not used internally more often is that they do not quickly dissolve in the body. They may become a semi-permanent fixture.

Happily, in the vast majority of cases there are no complications. For the first two or three days the patient is quite happy to sleep around the clock, waking only to eat. By the end of the week she is back in form, her stitches are removed, and the whole thing becomes a slightly nasty memory. After two or three weeks the hair is beginning to grow over the incision site and after another month you can hardly see where it was done.

The removal of the ovaries with all their hormones must obviously have other effects than simply stopping reproduction. Why, then, many people ask, don't veterinarians just remove the womb and one ovary and leave the other one intact?

Sometimes a part of an ovary is accidentally left behind. This usually occurs in very fat cats. The surgeon thinks he's removed an entire ovary but in fact a small portion is encased in the fat. Sometimes as he traces a branch of the uterus back to the ovary he exerts slightly too much pressure and it comes away in his hand, leaving the ovary behind. The ovary, a bit like a yo-yo on a string, slides back into position, where it may remain well and truly hidden. The veterinarian must then try and fish for it. As it's about the size of a pea and well away from the small incision he sometimes doesn't succeed. He may then decide to sew her up and see how she acts with that one ovary inside her. Almost always, such cats develop either urinary or sexual habits that prove embarrassing and inconvenient. Some in their frustration learn to spray. And not a few seem to be almost always on heat.

Does that answer the question? The solution is surgical. Somehow, whether it takes one hour or three, the veterinarian must open her up again and find the ovary and remove it.

The most common long-term side effects of the neutering operation in the female are very similar to those suffered by the neutered male. Top of the list is obesity. Although in theory it shouldn't make any difference, many owners find that it is easier to diet an overweight neutered female than it is to institute a similarly sensible regime for her fat brother. Either the neutered male is more beguiling and is sure to get his own way with his constant entreaties for food, or he is more independent and will have no hesitation in moving across to another more accommodating neighbour the first time the door is opened.

The female, even without her reproductive organs, either through greater dependence on her human keepers or (as some breeders claim) because of her innate superior intellect, will settle down after two or three days of resentment and accept what is given to her. Many veterinarians suggest that the amount of food be cut down gradually. One half an ounce should be sufficient for each pound of her normal weight. If she is meant to weigh eight or nine pounds, four or four and one-half ounces should be sufficient. On questioning owners we find that many cats of indolent habits are in fact eating a pound or pound and a half a day. The general idea is to cut the daily amount down by an ounce a week.

You mustn't of course carry this procedure too far. There is the story of the poor pedlar who kept reducing the amount of hay he fed his horse until after some months he was only feeding it a small handful a day. When the horse died the man said, 'It's a pity; another week and he would have been used to it.'

Although it may be slightly more expensive it's always a good idea to feed a dieting cat on top-quality food. One should avoid cereal fillers, too much fat, gravies, and sloppy tinned foods.

Almost always the veterinarian will dispense some vitamin mineral supplement to make sure that the creature doesn't develop some deficiency during the course of her diet. And as in the case of the male it may be necessary to partially replace the hormones elaborated by the ovaries with pills or injections.

Like her neutered brother, the spayed female's second great potential problem is a vast array of skin troubles. She has a wide variety of itches and baldnesses, each with its own name. These include summer eczemas, flea-bite dermatitis, hormonal alopecia, and enough etceteras to fill a whole book. Many of these can occur in the entire female, but somehow they always start with less cause in the neutered animal and become more severe. And in almost all cases replacement hormone therapy is indicated.

Some very few females are never right in the head after the operation. I have seen some possibly over-protected kittens that were so traumatized by even the minimal amount of handling necessary to anaesthetize them that they never again trusted a stranger.

Some, fortunately very few, are anaesthetized too deeply. For too many precious seconds the brain doesn't receive sufficient oxygen and it is permanently damaged. When I was a veterinary student we anaesthetized cats by the simple expedient of weighing them and giving them a capsule of appropriate strength. They took an hour or two to go down and then they stayed down for as long as twelve to twenty-four hours. The method was bad because once started it was impossible to control and basically only time could reverse it. In too many cases I suspect that the cat was too deep under for too long. This drug – which I won't name for fear of a suit for damages – is widely used on both sides of the ocean, even today. A professor of Veterinary Anaesthetics who has written one of the standard texts on the subject told me that in his opinion the drug was okay for euthanasia but definitely too dangerous to be used as an anaesthetic. Happily, during the past decade the message has spread and I know of few veterinary establishments which haven't switched to more modern and safer anaesthetics.

And finally, a percentage of neutered females develops neurological disorders after the operation for no apparent reason. As they almost always respond to treatment with replacement hormones, I must assume that the cause is the lack of those hormones.

Some veterinarians institute a course of treatment that will last for some six months. At the end of that time they gradually cut down the dosage and see if the patient can accommodate herself. If the symptoms recur they simply increase the dosage until they get her in balance. Some cats must stay on hormone drugs the rest of their lives.

A lot of people are puzzled because their neutered female remains as maternal as ever. Although she can't make milk, she loses no opportunity of mothering and protecting any strange youngsters, whether they be kittens, puppies, rabbits, or what have you. This phenomenon occurs particularly in Siamese, especially when they have already had a litter or two. This is additional proof that maternal (what the scientists prefer to call care-giving or epimeletic behaviour) love is not simply a matter of ovaries, uterus, and mammary glands. The brain's got a bit to do with it as well. Many females are spayed when they are nursing a litter of five, six, or eight weeks of age. The owner wants to spay them before they go out and get pregnant again. Many surprise their owners and themselves by continuing to give milk for many weeks after the operation. There is a scientific explanation for that, which includes the fact that the pituitary gland is a busy little gland. It's even busier than the ovaries. Another explanation is that somehow she knows that never again will she be able to have kittens. That explanation, I must hasten to add, has no scientific basis whatsoever. But who cares?

5 The Non-fertile Tom and Queen

THE NON-PERFORMING TOM

There are full-blown toms that would rather chase flies, sniff the morning air, eat, sleep or do nothing than participate in the sexual act. There are other toms that are enthusiastic about the idea and participate with vigour but are forced to retire in the feline equivalent of shame. Still others manage to perform adequately on most occasions and with honour on some but the results are not only negligible; they are non-existent.

In other words, there are three categories of tom that couldn't look old Charlie Darwin in the eye. There are those without sex drive; those with deficient sex drive; and those that are sterile.

Infuriatingly enough these are often the toms that because of their outstanding show characteristics would command the highest prices at stud. This may be because highly bred aristocrats are more prone to funny neuroses than the rest of us or it may be simply that one is more likely to make a fuss over a more valuable creature. If the stray tom around the corner suddenly decides he's had enough of the chase and would rather meditate in the sun people say what a comical creature he is and carry on with their knitting. If Blue Boy comes home from a triumphant show tour with a basketful of ribbons and promptly takes up sleep as a full-time occupation, absolutely refusing to wake up for a queen, everyone screams for the veterinarian.

There are probably as many sterile males as there are barren females. In the purebred-cat world we tend to notice them more because one male is expected to serve so many females. If he fails, the circle of dissappointed gossips is much larger than that which forms following the unsuccessful mating of a queen.

Let's deal first with the most common cause of impotence and infertility, the one which befalls every male of every species – if he doesn't die first. I refer to old age. Most scientists agree that the decline in sexual drive and performance which occurs in older animals is to a large extent genetically determined. Of course, if an older tom is fed badly or allowed to get ill or if his teeth are neglected you can expect him to lose condition and sexual interest earlier.

This non-fertility of old age is a problem that can be tackled by the breeder and the veterinarian with a clear conscience. They are not trying to promulgate a weak line full of abnormalities. They are trying to reproduce the characteristics the tom possessed in his vigorous youth, and although it may be more difficult for the old boy there is no reason to suppose that the kittens he sires in older life will be inferior to those he sired previously. I know that some studies on humans show that middle-aged females have a slightly increased percentage of abnormal babies but there's no evidence that the same thing occurs in animals. It may be relevant to point out here that many thoroughbred stallions only begin their breeding careers after they have completed their life on the tracks. It would be interesting to compile a list of famous colts that were sired by retired fathers of ten or more.

How can one lengthen the effective breeding life of an ageing tom? First, take him along to the veterinarian for a thorough checkup. Infected ears, decayed teeth, ingrowing claws, impacted anal glands, a matted coat, a chronic discharging eye, and persistent nasal discharge are all typical minor conditions with which the middle-aged cat can cope but the elderly one cannot. These easily treated conditions won't affect the fertility of a middle-aged tom (although they won't do him any good) but they are sufficient to stop an elderly tom from performing.

Sometimes the old tom just loses interest. That gleam can often be partially restored by a hormone injection. The veterinarian will usually suggest trying one injection or two and if it is effective in restoring his interest allow him to mount a proven queen. The tom may be deficient not only in sex drive – he may be sterile as well. Under those circumstances there is no point in restoring his interest if he's going to be incapable of producing kittens. If he does mate the selected queen successfully, however, the veterinarian may agree to insert a wax or oil pellet of hormone under his skin. There it will release its benefits for approximately six months.

Of course you mustn't overwork an ageing tom; nor can you fairly ask him to sap his energies struggling with an inexperienced, unwilling, or vicious female.

Finally I must point out that the ancient Arabian belief that a jaded appetite may be completely revived, albeit temporarily, by a supply of fresh females has been given scientific corroboration in at least four species of animal. The guinea pig, the rat, the hamster, and the bull all apparently get a bit bored with the same old female. When experimenters substitute a fresh female on heat the males that were responding poorly very quickly react by bouncing back to a response of maximum intensity. (As one group of scientists put it, 'sexual satiation to one stimulus provides negligible interference with a subsequent response to a new stimulus animal'.) I have not read about any similar experiments using cats, but even without the discipline of controlled experiments I am sure one could fairly say that many toms find it a pleasant change to be greeted by a fresh face.

All those measures and more can do no harm but, as any used-car dealer can tell you, an engine has only got so much life in it no matter how many times you turn back the speedometer.

Among domesticated cats – particularly among purebred show cats – youth is not without its problems. Toms that have been reared in relative isolation are frequently frightened by the sight of another cat. Even after several hours of exposure to a female on heat in an adjoining cage their sexual drive often cannot overcome their social timidity. Sometimes these shy toms can be helped by introducing them to some friendly pet cats in a non-sexual atmosphere. They need to learn first of all how to behave with other animals. Once they learn that others are not a threat they may then be introduced to an experienced female in oestrus. It is extremely important that on the first occasion, and preferably the next half dozen as well, the male be allowed to mate the female in his own familiar home territory. It would be the height of folly to expect such a male to successfully conquer and mount a nervous or aggressive female. One should use a placid, experienced queen. If his timidity seems to bring out her latent aggressiveness she may be given a tranquillizer like potassium bromide, phenobarbitone, or one of the chlorpromazines. Most veterinarians agree that it is ethical to dispense a half dozen or a dozen of each of those drugs to a breeder who is known to them. They know and the breeder knows that they won't be used unnecessarily. And the dosage in cats is so small that should the whole envelope fall into the wrong hands it could scarcely do any harm. The veterinarian will usually warn the breeder that tranquillizers have variable effects on cats. You don't give a pill to a cat and then shove her in with another. It may have the opposite of the intended effect. Every veterinary establishment has had the extremely unpleasant experience of trying to restrain a cat that has gone beserk on what should have been a safe dose of tranquillizer. I repeat. You should test each queen with the tranquillizer you intend using before introducing her to a shy or inexperienced tom.

Some young toms that have been confined in unsuitable cages for long periods may literally go insane. I think the term 'stircrazy' is apt. A cat may be confined for a week or two or even three in cramped quarters without adequate light or ventilation without apparent damage. After a month, in my experience, they definitely begin to deteriorate. They lose interest. They go off their food. If they're kept cramped for a further month many of them could not face a mouse with equanimity and a female cat, particularly one in oestrus, would send them cowering behind the nearest shelter.

Purebred cats in the main must be confined to cages, but those cages should include both an outdoor run and a verandah on which the cat can, if he chooses, lie or pace outdoors sheltered from the elements. The outdoor run should be so situated that the imprisoned creature can bask in the sun. The outdoor run should also contain a ledge, because many cats prefer to observe the passing scene from on high. Some breeders have found that it pays dividends to allow their budding stud a companion or two. Usually the companion is a neutered cat. Many people find that Persian cats and Pekingese dogs get along well together. (This may mean no more than the fact that the same sort of people are attached to both sorts of animals. They like hair.) Others find the dachshunds get along with all sorts of cats. I do know that many of them adopt the most catlike postures and I know of no other breed of dog that manages to look so much like a cat when it's cleaning itself.

The humans who attend to the needs of a caged animal should be firmly reminded that although it may be more efficient to do all the necessary chores in one short burst it is a much better policy to split those duties throughout the entire day. There is a vast literature describing the feelings of human prisoners and we have no reason to assume that many of their reactions aren't applicable to animals. And how many times in this prison literature are we told that the captive measures his hours by the appearance of the warder?

There are many other psychological reasons why a tom may go off the idea of sex. These are less common in the middle-aged experienced tom because once he gets an established taste for copulation it takes quite a trauma to put him off. The younger, less sure tom reacts more severely to slighter knocks.

That knock may be as simple as an overly heavy or cumbersome harness. In fact some toms refuse to 'work' if they are wearing any form of incumbrance.

Too much light will put some toms off. All but the most virile of males find the steady interruptions of camera flashbulbs distracting. A young inexperienced tom could end up really confused.

Sometimes after a really bad mauling by a female a tom will go off the whole damn lot of them. This, as some of us have discovered, time will heal.

There are dozens of physical – as opposed to psychological or hereditary – factors that may lower the potency or interest of a tom. The one met with most commonly is an injury or an infection of the testicle, usually received during a fight with another cat. Such an injury may also be caused by awkward falls, glancing blows from automobiles, and sharp kicks inflicted by humans or cows. (Had you forgotten that many cats like to attend milking sessions?)

External applications are both difficult to apply and of questionable value, and usually the cat will lick them off. The injuries are very painful and often the veterinarian will decide that they are serious enough to necessitate an injection of a cortico-steroid. Some veterinarians use injections of a pain-killer called pethidine.

If the injury becomes infected or if the testicles swell as a result of the spread of the infection, a course of antibiotics may be indicated.

The tom will probably be acutely ill and uninterested in everything including food for at least three days, possibly as long as a week, but as the injections begin to take effect he will once more take an interest in life. No matter how well he appears most veterinarians will advise a sexual rest of a month.

Sometimes one of the testicles is so badly torn or infected that it has to be removed in order to save the life of the cat. After he has fully recovered from the operation he will be as good as ever. The loss of one testicle will not affect his breeding performance; nor will it upset any show judges, provided they are shown a veterinary certificate proving that the condition was caused by surgery and not heredity. In many cases, however, both testicles must be removed, and the animal's breeding life is finished.

Sometimes a tom refuses a queen because he is ill. Fair enough. When he's cured, convalesced, and recuperated his interest should revive.

Sometimes he's just too fat and lazy. After a couple of months on a supervised diet the new slim Sam should be anxious to get back to work.

The vast majority of non-virile toms presented to veterinarians, however, are those that are just plain not interested. They never have been and without injections they never will be. These toms may be Nature's way of saying to breeders, 'Look, you've gone just about as far as you can go with this particular bit of refined nonsense.'

The two examples that occur to me are both Rex toms. These are the so-called woolly cats, which currently command very high prices. The Rex was a natural mutation which occurred in south-west England in the 1950's. The characteristic tight fuzzy coat was fixed by inbreeding and soon two sorts of Rex breed were well established. Today there are hundreds of Rex cats. A sizable minority have no coat at all (hairless cats), a lot of them are very difficult to rear, and some of the toms refuse to breed. Why do I go into this aside about Rex cats, knowing full well that irate breeders will write nasty letters? They'll tell me I haven't the faintest idea of what I'm talking about, that their Rex cats all have terrific thick woolly coats, they're easier to rear than ordinary cats(in fact one breeder in response to a newspaper article wrote saying that his Rex cats were the only ones that survived an epidemic that swept through his cattery), and that all their toms are virile and fertile beyond belief. They'll further threaten to sue me for libel and suggest I'm taking the meat out of their cats' mouths.

Ah yes! That's the way it is for them. But in my limited experience with the breed I ran into a lot with little or no hair, a lot that die early; and I've run into two toms that couldn't be enticed to mount a queen. May I repeat that it may be one of Nature's ways of saying, 'You've carried this nonsense quite far enough.'

Finally there is one other reason why a tom refuses a queen. He's had too many and just wants a rest.

THE BARREN QUEEN

Veterinarians don't spend a great deal of time worrying about female cats that can't have kittens. The vast majority of their clients are far more concerned about cats that do have kittens than those that don't. Only rarely does the owner of a particularly valuable (or treasured albeit valueless) cat insist that everything possible should be done to get her pregnant. And as happens so often in the human world, Nature manages to mix everything up. Those that wish to get pregnant can't; those that don't give a slight thought in that direction can and do.

In many species of animal the commonest causes of infertility in the female are sickness, obesity, and age. The problem of illness can only be properly dealt with by a veterinarian. I'm not saying that as a profession we are perfect or even nearly so. Outside of myself and a few close friends I can think of hardly anyone who falls into that category. But as most veterinarians are of at least average intelligence and as they have all spent some years studying the field and many more years practising in it, you can expect them to know a bit more than someone who has signed a lease on a business site and put in a stock of herbal remedies.

I have an axe to grind and I intend to grind it. People who love cats often believe in such admirable concepts as vegetarianism, exercise and fresh air, the evils of tobacco, the virtues of compost heaps and whole grain bread, and madrigals. Cats also include among their admirers more than their fair share of spiritualists, faith healers, and those who believe that a pain in a tooth can be cured by an infusion of leaves. I have had direct experience with two men who have made a great deal of profit peddling their lies to innocent cat owners. One is a man who claims to heal by the laying on of hands.

Many is the cat that has felt them; and I admit that it does no direct harm. But when that man's old parrot developed an infection, the faith healer was quite happy to accept my prescription for antibiotics.

The other man owns a large wholesale business which purveys herbal remedies to animal owners on both sides of the ocean. At every major dog and cat show in England he has an impressive stand and several articulate sales ladies, all of whom can go into the greatest detail about the miraculous cures effected by the tiny packages of mixed vegetable matter. That man's wife has a chronic lung condition. Does he use his own herbs to treat it? Don't be foolish! He's got lots of money and can afford the best. The doctor she sees wouldn't know a herb from a weed.

Aside from bilking the public these people do a great deal of harm in that a condition that might have been easily treated in its early stages is often allowed to become complicated and incurable. Also, of course, very often the poor animal is in considerable pain while proper treatment is available around the corner.

What bearing does all this have on the subject of infertility in the female cat? One fairly common condition that occurs in growing kittens is cystitis, or an infection of the bladder. It may occur for any one of a half a dozen reasons or for none that is apparent. Sometimes the kitten picks up a little infection around its vaginal orifice and it spreads. The signs include itchiness, irritability, rubbing of the bottom along a harsh surface, and often repeated visits to the litter tray. Quite commonly owners mistake these signs for constipation. Almost as commonly they pick up some remedy for it at the shop. Only after the illness has continued for several days or sometimes weeks do they consult a veterinarian who clears it up very quickly with any one of the twenty or thirty modern drugs available for the purpose. The point is that in a sizeable percentage of neglected cases the infection doesn't remain in the bladder. It can travel upwards and cause extremely serious damage to the kidneys or permanent damage to the womb.

That is only one example of a neglected minor illness that can lead to permanent infertility. There are, of course, many illnesses that despite all professional treatment result in permanent damage to the reproductive system. More of that later.

Overweight females – and for that matter overweight males – do not function as well as their more normal relatives. They can't run or hunt as well. When they climb they wheeze and when they sleep they snore. And, when it comes time to reproduce themselves, they always find it more difficult than do their slimmer friends. Some of them find it impossible!

Among purebred cats one meets the problem of obesity more often in the Long-haired (Persian) cats than among Domestic Short-haired cats or Orientals. I know that they are meant to be blocky, well muscled, and thick through the chest with plenty of capacity, but some of them are absolutely ridiculous. Like too many dachshunds, they couldn't walk across a wet road without getting their tummies damp.

At the other end of the weight scale we occasionally see animals that because of severe emaciation don't mature properly or fail to come into heat. Some veterinarians who have only practised in the English-speaking parts of the world have happily never seen such a case.

Some cats that are kept locked away from males for the first year or year and a half of their lives appear to be so messed up by this artificial deprivation that they refuse to accept the tom when finally they are allowed one. Sometimes a tranquillizer lowers their resistance. Sometimes the delay produces more serious damage. These cats appear to cycle in a normal fashion but they don't become pregnant. After a few attempts the owners agree to have them neutered. Almost invariably the uterus turns out to be swollen, inflamed, or partially filled with mucus or pus.

I am told by a doctor friend of mine who has a very busy gynaecological practice that women who delay having children until their late twenties often have difficulty conceiving. Strangely enough, he says, by the late thirties and early forties the difficulties seem to disappear and once again conception becomes easy. Maybe by the same token if maiden cats were given another year or two before trying again conception would be more likely to occur.

Some cats are sterile because they were born with a defect in the reproductive system. Sometimes they are born without any sign of the horns of the uterus. The external opening is normal and so apparently is the vagina and, because the kidneys and bladder and so on are all perfectly normal, the kitten grows up living a completely normal existence. She does have a uterus and ovaries, but she simply doesn't come into heat. This condition is so rare that most busy veterinarians have never seen a case.

Slightly more common are female kittens born with just one horn on the uterus. The incidence of this condition is put at something like one in a thousand. Such kittens will come on heat normally and if mated will conceive, but they never seem to have more than one or two kittens. The cat does not appear to suffer at all from the condition, and I suppose, in its way, this built-in birth control can be considered a blessing.

I once inadvertently produced such an abnormality. About halfway through a spaying operation, the patient suffered a respiratory failure. When one ovary and horn were out of the cavity, I decided to tie it off and devote all my efforts to restoring normal breathing. That took several long moments and the kitten, instead of coming around gradually, seemed to come fully awake in a second. I couldn't take a chance and re-anaesthetize at that particular juncture, so I hurriedly sutured the peritoneum and then the skin. When the owners came to collect the kitten I told them exactly what had happened.

'We'll wait a few weeks to let her get over that,' I said, 'and then we'll do her again.'

'Oh, no, you won't,' said the owners. 'We were against this from the beginning and this is a sure sign that it shouldn't have been done.'

I protested that we simply couldn't leave her like that – I tried to explain to them that all sorts of fearful things might happen to their cat if they left her half spayed. I don't know whether I was trying to convince them or myself. In any event, I was wrong.

A few months later they brought her in for a pre-mating check-up. When she was pronounced normal in all respects except the one we are discussing they agreed that the easiest way to have her mated would be to simply open the back door some warm evening. This they did, and three weeks later she came in and was pronounced unmistakably pregnant. Because of her history, we decided to check her every week. There were no problems but not unexpectedly she never did get really very full. At the end of sixty-four or sixty-five days (we can't say which because she was let out on two successive nights) she produced two perfectly normal kittens of average size. She raised them without any difficulty.

She continued to produce a litter of two, twice a year, for a further four years. She had barely weaned her sixth litter when she got killed by the common enemy, which doesn't differentiate between races, colours, creeds, or species. How would you describe a motor-car?

Some of the other anatomic or congenital defects or abnormalities found in the reproductive system of female cats include hermaphroditism (but this is very rare and almost always the male dominates), a shrunken vagina (so small to be almost non-existent and of course non-functioning), and other such rarities. Considering the thousands of cell divisions necessary to produce even the simplest organ, the wonder is not that the odd one goes wrong but that the overwhelming majority are invariably right.

Infertility may also result from a disturbance of the hormone flow. One of the more common examples of this type of infertility is caused by cysts on the ovary. There is another sort that is usually seen in elderly cats and is almost always associated with an inflammation or a thickening of the uterus. The cat may produce several litters without trouble and then when she reaches about six or seven or eight years of age, without any apparent illness, she stops cycling into season. Or, if she does come on heat and accepts the male, she either fails to conceive or miscarries very early. Injections of hormones occasionally help but are really just a temporary measure. Even the most ambitious breeder with the most valuable queen will usually accept this as Nature's sign that she has done her bit, and agree to have her spayed.

Another sort of cyst, which occasionally occurs in younger cats, may result in nymphomania. Affected cats are almost always sterile, and in addition they are usually nervous and occasionally vicious. Some cats work themselves up to such a state because of their constant insatiable sexual demands that they have fits. It seems the height of cruelty not to have such pitiful creatures spayed.

May I ask readers to remember before rushing into a diagnosis of nymphomania in their own cats that many Orientals act pretty sexy when they're having an ordinary heat. Remember, too, that they will stay in heat for ten days if there is no male around and about two weeks later go through the whole screaming procedure again. Some authorities suggest that an injection of a hormone called chorionic gonadotropin at the beginning of this heat period would shorten it to three or four days. The disadvantages are that, first, it's quite an expensive injection, second, one is faced with the whole business again in a few weeks, and

third, one shouldn't mess around with hormones unnecessarily.

Some cats have enough hormones of the right sort to come on season and to get pregnant but not enough to maintain pregnancy. They miscarry. Some veterinarians have successfully treated this condition with injections of a hormone called progesterone, which they give twice weekly up to the last week of pregnancy. After the cat has had one litter she is often able to have another one normally without the aid of injections.

Sometimes a cat has one or more normal litters and then seems to be unable to conceive. The most common cause is an infection or an injury which has not cleared up from the last time she had a litter. She may have managed to produce the kittens on her own but severely bruised her birth canal in the process. Sometimes a kitten actually tears the canal as it's being born. If it's a small laceration there's usually a bit of haemorrhage but then it heals quite nicely on its own. But if it's a large tear, or a jagged one, or in an awkward position it remains as an open draining sore and prevents further pregnancy. Sometimes a bit of afterbirth has been left over and acts a bit like an intra-uterine device in women.

In most cases, of course, such conditions produce an acutely ill cat within days of their occurrence. She'll go off her food, her temperature will go up, she won't be able to milk her kittens, and she may have a smelly bloody discharge. The veterinarian must decide whether antibiotics will be effective or whether surgery is necessary.

The acute form, as described above, is noticed by even the most casual owner. It is the chronic form which may escape notice. It is really quite remarkable that the cat can suffer a vaginal or uterine infection, which would prove fatal to any other sort of animal, without any apparent ill effects. Only when she is taken to the veterinarian to find out why she is infertile is the condition discovered.

Some cats are incapable of becoming pregnant because they have a cyst, an abscess, or a tumour in the vagina. The veterinarian will bathe the abscess, drain it, and give an injection or two or three of antibiotics, and in nine cases out of ten the cat should then conceive without difficulty. Cysts, provided they're not too deep, are usually easily removed surgically. They seldom recur. And fortunately, most of the tumours found in this region of the cat turn out to be benign. After careful excision and several weeks of observation to make sure that the site heals nicely and that there is no re-growth of the tumour she can be safely mated.

There may be other causes of infertility to add to that depressing list but you need not worry because they're not included here. Your veterinarian has got a great big thick book which doesn't miss one. And if by some chance the phone doesn't ring one evening he's going to read it.

6 The Pre-mating Check-up

A pre-mating checkup need be neither tedious nor expensive. During the course of a fifteen-minute examination the veterinarian will concentrate on six potential sources of trouble: worms; fleas, lice and other external parasites; ear mites; flu; enteritis and obvious nutritional deficiencies. An adult female may suffer from any one or all of these without appearing unduly ill to the inexperienced eye. Her kittens, however, will almost certainly be affected and their development will be retarded. Cats have managed to procreate without the aid of medical science for thousands of years, but their kittens have often suffered from ailments that could have easily been prevented.

The presence of worms is not usually easy to detect solely by the appearance of the cat. Often the only external signs are a dry starey coat, a slightly potbellied look, and occasional bouts of coughing or digestive upsets. Sometimes a cat will appear in blooming health despite a heavy infestation. She may, however, bring up an occasional round worm. These are thin and long and round. When they die and dry they sometimes look like flattened string with a wavy reddish line down the middle. Sometimes an apparently healthy cat will pass a few segments of tape worm in her motion. These, when dry, look a bit like individual grains of rice.

In the absence of any of these signs the veterinarian may ask for a sample of the cat's motion. Don't let this casually uttered request send you chasing down back alleys for a week or more without success. It's often simpler to lock the cat up until she decides that a litter tray isn't really all that repugnant. You can help overcome her hesitation by feeding a meal of raw liver. It's natural, nutritious, delicious, laxative and cheap.

The veterinarian will mix the sample with salt water, spin it down in a centrifuge or allow it to slowly settle out in a test tube. Under the microscope the worm eggs can easily be seen. Each sort of worm lays its own sort of egg, and the cat is treated accordingly.

You cannot be casual about worms in the potential mother. They deplete her at a time when all her reserves are being used to feed the developing embryos. And obviously kittens born to a worm-infested mother are more likely to get worms than those born to one that has been properly treated. That means professional treatment by the veterinarian, and not with pet shop cathartics or garlic capsules from the health herbarium.

Get a strong light, a steady table, and a scratchproof assistant to search a cat for fleas or lice. Fleas are small and brown and move quickly. With patience you can see individual fleas scurrying away from the light. Sometimes you won't see the flea, but only the black specks which are their excrement. Lice usually look like bits of cigarette ash. Watch carefully and you will see the moving individuals that compose the mass. Sometimes one can see the tiny lice nits which are strung along an individual cat hair.

There are many products on the market which will kill the fleas or lice. Make sure to buy one labelled 'Safe for Cats'.

Whatever sort you use, brush it out thoroughly, because otherwise the cat while cleansing itself may swallow enough to injure its liver permanently. Remember that a product made to kill insects cannot possibly be entirely safe for any living creature.

The whole dusting or spraying procedure may have to be repeated two or three times at weekly intervals. In the case of fleas the whole area which the cat occupies must be sprayed at the same time, not only because the eggs may be resistant to the spray or powder but also because some of the adult fleas may have decided to take the afternoon off. After you've finished dusting and grooming your cat they happily return.

Sometimes in old houses spraying may not be sufficient. A heavy infestation may call for the services of a professional fumigator.

Some people believe that with the advent of deterrent 'flea collars' and hanging strips of impregnated material designed to kill all insects in the area such old-fashioned methods are no longer necessary. Many of them work, I agree – but at what price? A colleague of mine works in the animal colony at a cancer laboratory. Scientists being scientists, they couldn't resist running an insect-control programme on the side, using both collars and strips. The 'protected' animals had a mortality rate one third higher than those that were not! Until the manufacturers come up with proof to the contrary I'll rid my cat of fleas in the old-fashioned ways.

Why do I go into such detail about creatures that are usually considered more a nuisance than a major problem? Because there are few more pitiful sights than a litter of helpless kittens, a few hours or days old, whose every crevice is occupied by marauding parasites. It surely must be cruelty to bring creatures into a world where the first sensation after hunger must be a constant and unrelievable irritation, when we can so easily prevent it all by a few moments' attention to the mother and her environs. (Many people are convinced that newborn creatures, including humans, are so insensitive that they don't notice insects crawling into their eyes or ears, but strangely enough no one disagrees that even the gentlest of insecticides seems to upset tiny kittens. Once they are infested it becomes a very difficult task to cleanse them.)

Possibly the most distressing feature of flea-ridden newborn kittens is the fact that the concentration always seems to be heaviest around the eyes. One picks the fleas off one by one and returns an apparently clean kitten to the mother only to find it covered again a few moments later.

During the pre-mating checkup the veterinarian will have a careful look inside the cat's ears. A dark brown or blackish discharge or encrustation is typical of an ear-mite infection. These crawlers, which can be easily seen with a low-power glass, are called Notoedres species by the scientist. They live on the lining of the ear. The discharge is the ear's attempt to rid itself of the foreign irritation.

Treatment of the condition is normally very easy. The veterinarian will show you how he pours a liquid medicine into the ear, gives the base of the ear a gentle massage, and gently wipes away the mixture of discharge and medicine which rises. The procedure is repeated three or four times with each ear. Inevitably the cat will try to help after a few seconds by shaking his head. The black blobs fly everywhere. That's the reason a lot of veterinarians wear spectacles. The cat also tries to help by scratching with its hind feet. That's why the veterinarian asks you to hold your cat while he stands well back.

Generally one doesn't repeat the procedure more than twice a week. It is the experience of many cat breeders that any handling or treatment of the ears repeated more often than this may set up its own irritation. During the interval your hands will have a good chance to heal and you can pop down to the launderette with your soiled clothes.

Mild cases should be cured after four or five cleansings. More serious ones might take a couple or three more. Surely that's not too much effort to make to prevent a kitten from being exposed to infection at a tender and vulnerable age.

Yet another common problem in adult cats that may all too easily be passed on to the newborn kitten is that of flu and all its complications. Unless a flu is treated vigorously and thoroughly (which is to say professionally) from the outset the cat is more than likely to be left with a chronic case of snuffles or sinusitis or bronchitis or worse. Sometimes despite the best treatment available one gets the same unhappy results. This usually happens in a home with three or more cats. The reason is that the infection is no sooner cleared up in one than it breaks out in another. This ping-pong situation can go on for months. That is why many veterinarians today insist on treating all of the cats in a household even if only one is showing signs of flu.

If you have a catless relative (preferably one who is also neither blessed with children nor dogs) he may possibly be prevailed upon to accept one of the cats until the outbreak is over. In my experience, this simple move is often as effective as more elaborate measures. Dogless, childless people are best for this temporary nursing adoption because, like ourselves, a sick animal wants quiet and privacy. Then, too, we now know that many dozens of viruses capable of causing flu in human beings can successfully invade the cat. And vice versa. The less people about the less chance the virus has for a game of ping-pong.

We still do not know whether flu viruses travel between dogs and cats. I suspect that as our veterinary scientists delve deeper they will prove that there are some flu viruses that couldn't care less whether their host is called Rover or Tigerlily.*

It is a fact that many nursing cats that suffer only mildly with the after effects of a flu can pass the virus on to their kittens. Sometimes the kittens come down with it while they are still nursing. More often they go through the initial five weeks without problems, but as they are weaned the virus seems to get an upper hand. That is why during the pre-mating checkup the veterinarian will sometimes take a nasal or a throat swab. This is cultured and then tested to see which antibiotics would be most effective in getting rid of the infection once and for all. This usually works quite nicely if only bacteria are involved. But if, as is so often the case, the primary case is a virus and if the cat can't seem to shake it off you must seriously ask if you are doing the right thing by mating the cat at that time.

In the case of purebred cats which may have to be transported to the stud you must also ask if it is fair to introduce an infection to other premises. It is surprising how many breeders will dose up their queen with antibiotics in order to temporarily suppress the symptoms of a chronic sinusitus and then feign complete innocence when a couple of weeks later the owner of the stud complains that all her cats are sneezing!

The fifth villain is the killer disease called feline infectious enteritis in England and (more properly) feline panleukopenia in America. The veterinarian will want to have a look at the queen's certification of inoculation. He may consider that it is time for a booster. Although it is still a controversial question as to whether and to what degree nursing kittens can pick up immunity to the disease from their mother's milk, we do

* An example of this constant shifting of the scientific horizon is the recent report that dogs could catch Psitticosis from budgerigars and parrots. For fifty years or so we have known that this bird disease could cause a particularly nasty pneumonia in the human being. It was never thought that the disease travelled through dogs until an alert investigator in Edinburgh visited a home where the budgerigars were dying and the people had Psitticosis pneumonia. He noticed that the dog was coughing. X-rays showed the extent of its pneumonia and laboratory investigation proved that it had been caused by Psitticosis.

know that the vaccine is both safe and effective. I have yet to hear of a case where a booster inoculation did any harm. Most people agree that if more than a year has elapsed since the last inoculation or if the certificate has been lost or indeed one was never produced then it's better to damn the expense and subject the poor creature to the indignity of yet another needle.

The problem of missing certificates is an ever-recurring one. Many shoddy dealers and a very few shabby breeders swear by all their holy cash registers that the kitten they are selling is wormed, vetted, inoculated, vaccinated, certificated, registered, and double-pedigreed when in fact they don't know the first thing about it.

Every veterinarian should, and most of them do, make out a certificate at the time the inoculation is completed. They also keep a duplicate. If a certificate cannot be produced there is no reason why a copy cannot be obtained. Some vendors will claim that they do their kittens themselves. They say that they have a source of vaccine and a syringe and there's nothing to it! The answer to that must be that if the kitten is worth X pounds it surely must be worth X plus a few pounds more to make sure it's done properly. Should a certificated cat come down with a disease which looks suspiciously like panleukopenia both the veterinarian who signed the certificate and the firm who manufactured the vaccine will consider that it is very much their responsibility.

Sometimes it turns out to be something far less serious. Sometimes one discovers that the cat is one of that rare minority that is incapable of producing antibodies. Sometimes, rarely, a whole bath of vaccine turns out to be ineffective. And sometimes one never discovers why the unfortunate cat comes down with the disease.

In most cases where the vendor claims to have inoculated the cat or claims that the cat was inoculated previously one has no way of tracing back exactly what may have happened. Sometimes the lay vaccinator uses a syringe which has been rinsed in alcohol. Sometimes the vaccine is past date and sometimes it has not been kept refrigerated. Sometimes the needle doesn't penetrate the skin. Some times it goes in one side and out the other. These and a dozen other errors of ignorance or avarice may leave a supposedly immune cat susceptible to a horrible death.

Why not simplify your life and insure that of your cat and her kittens by asking your veterinarian?

Finally to the experienced professional eye a single glance during this pre-mating check-up may be sufficient to diagnose a nutritional fault. It is a sad commentary on the way man manages his affairs that widespread famine exists in two continents while in the other two the most common nutritional disease seen in pets is obesity.

Part II
PREGNANCY AND BIRTH

1 The Pregnant Cat

During the first three weeks of pregnancy the cat appears unchanged. Rarely does she suffer spells of nausea; nor does she display signs of pleased accomplishment. She jumps, hunts, and lazes with the same effortless grace as ever. Her interests and indifferences remain the same.

If it is her first pregnancy her nipples may become pink, enlarged, and tenderly erect from about the sixteenth day. About the end of the third week of pregnancy the developing lives within her may be felt – by the experienced hand – gently. At that age they feel like pea-sized bumps within the uterus. A week later they have grown into tense balls about an inch thick. At this stage they are still easily felt as separate units. A few days later they become larger, softer, and less round and one can no longer feel them individually.

Not until the fifth or even sixth week of pregnancy do most cats become visibly swollen. At seven weeks the experienced veterinarian can often feel the outline of individual kittens. At that stage the kittens have enough bone development to show on X-ray. Before then they would appear as shadows on the film, if they show at all.

During the final week the pregnant cat may become slower and more cautious in her movements. Some – usually those carrying litters of six or more – become very full. They may surprise themselves by moving awkwardly for the first time since kittenhood and (depending upon the temperament of the owner) produce reactions of amusement or concern.

If she's not dependent on a particular human she becomes interested in corners and hideaways. Although she doesn't actually build a nest as do so many birds she does finally choose a particular place in which to have her young. She chooses an ill-lit, private, dry, draught-free place if such is available. She makes herself familiar with its faults and its virtues. She pays particular regard to its accesses and egresses. She spends hours lying in it. Its odour becomes her odour.

Breast development becomes pronounced during the last few days. Gentle squeezing may bring a drop of milk a day or sometimes three before term. Occasionally she may produce a fair bit of milk before kittening but so long as the breasts are not visibly sore or painful to the touch no treatment is necessary. She grooms over and around her breasts by the hour. She smooths the hair away from the nipples. Some long-haired cats pluck the hair from the area. If she doesn't do it properly the owner must carefully trim it away, because it can interfere with nursing.

Nice neat tables of gestation periods state that the cat carries its young for an average of sixty-three days. As a result veterinarians get panic phone calls on that day or the next reporting that 'she's not showing any signs of anything but gluttony'. Provided she's acting normally and eating one need not worry. Many, many cats go sixty-six days, and I know of several queens with recorded dates of mating that have gone sixty-seven. One Siamese I know went that long. She got bigger and bigger and bigger. One wondered how one small lithe creature could stretch so round. From the sixty-fifth day she had a daily veterinary examination. The anxious owners wondered whether it wouldn't be better to induce labour with an injection. But apart from her size and awkwardness she appeared so well that it was decided to watch and wait. Then, during the night of the sixty-eighth day and into the sixty-ninth she produced a litter of ten! As you might expect she was very tired. During the long night she had delivered at the rate of a kitten an hour. Between times she gave suckle and rested as best she could. When she was finally finished she slept for three hours, then ate a light meal of flaked boiled cod and complainingly asked for more. And, incidentally, she had no difficulty rearing the entire litter. She could never have done so had her owners not followed instructions. The kittens started supplemental feeding when they were a mere two-and-a-half weeks old. And needless to say the proud mother got nothing but the best or better.

How should one feed a cat through her pregnancy? Provided she's being fed properly one need make no startling changes during the first three weeks.

Many household cats are provided with a light breakfast of milk or milk with a bit of cereal or sometimes milk and egg. Some, particularly Orientals, reject milk soon after kittenhood. In fact I know some that will reject any breakfast however tempting if they even vaguely suspect that it was designed for cats, not people. Such cats will take anything including cornflakes or even orange juice provided it's presented from their owner's table and not in a bowl on the floor. These present a special problem and I'll return to them later.

Most cats, even the most spoiled, are not quite so choosy about their supper. This main meal of the day should be fed about the same time each day and it should consist of meat (raw or cooked), chicken (cooked and boned) or fish (cooked and boned and preferably not more than twice a week).

Cats that are fed too much fish suffer from skin disorders more often than those that have a varied diet. That is not to say that there are not many healthy and sleek cats that eat nothing but fish, but on the average those on fish diets get skin trouble more often and they get it more seriously, and it's much more difficult to treat.

Tinned food is perfectly okay provided it is properly labelled. Otherwise one has to guess whether the cat is getting meat or stodgy cereal topped up with a bit of gravy.

The best commercial cat foods have two advantages. Firstly they are convenient. They are of even consistency. Bones are either removed or ground. They are readily available and easily stored. They come in appropriate sizes. Secondly their formulae are drawn up by professional nutritionists. Although they must work within rigid economic requirements and despite the fact that they must produce a product which is palatable in appearance to its human buyers (a factor that the cat cares about little if at all), they still manage to balance the stuff with the right proteins, vitamins, and minerals. Choose carefully among the labelled products. Generally, but not always, price corresponds with quality. Stock up with a couple of dozen tins of two or three different sorts. Choose one of the biscuit or meal types as well. Get a large package.

In addition you'll need to buy a pound or two of feeding bonemeal and about one hundred mixed vitamin tablets as prescribed by your veterinarian. The bonemeal is for calcium. The vitamin tablets are primarily for vitamins A and D but will contain the others as well. Some veterinarians prefer to dispense a tablet which contains all the needed minerals and vitamins. You must not depend on the well advertised and ubiquitous yeast-base tablets, which provide little more than vitamins of the B group. These are never harmful, and often do a lot of good, but they are not nearly so important for the pregnant and nursing cat as are calcium and vitamins A and D. It is false economy to neglect those essential supplements. Remember too that one can do more harm than good by giving too many. Too much vitamin A or D particularly is worse than too little. Don't get upset or make it complicated. Just follow your veterinarian's instructions.

You can inaugurate a simple feeding regime like the following. Three or four or five days of the week, provide a fair-sized dinner (about half an ounce for every pound that the cat weighs) of meat or chicken. Use fish instead on one or two days if the cat is particularly fond of it and if you don't mind preparing it. Each of these meals must be topped up with bonemeal, a vitamin tablet, or both. You can, of course, use good quality leftovers and you should add a bit of acceptable vegetables (either raw or cooked) from your own table. (Remember that cats need and relish tender grass or the digesting greens inside their prey). The other two or three days of the week (when you're too busy to bother) use the tinned stuff. If these contain more than five per cent ground bone then you need not add bonemeal. You should still mix in the vitamin supplement. Although the tinned foods should contain sufficient vitamins for the normal cat they may not contain enough for the added needs of pregnancy and lactation.

Many people believe that it's absolute nonsense to remove all the bones from the cat's food and then replace it in the form of bonemeal or calcium tablets. After all, they say, the cat throughout its history has relished bones – particularly those of birds. That's true. And I know of many cats that can purposefully grind their way through any skeleton. But I also know of many others that have been rushed to the veterinarian's because a piece of bone has lodged in the teeth, the throat, or further down out of reach of everything but the surgical scalpel. And neither I nor anyone else has any idea of the number of untended cats that have come to an untimely and painful death as the result of a bone. Obviously not every cat that eats the occasional bone is going to die of it or even suffer, and many digest bones regularly and happily. My cat Malcolm would eat a human foot – boot and all – if he were given the opportunity. But sure as taxes as soon as you tell a person that it is okay to feed their cat or dog on bones they'll bring the creature in the following week for a post-mortem and you'll pick out a piece of bone that caused the fatal obstruction.

The pregnant cat should be encouraged to take breakfast. Although previously she may have been perfectly content on one meal a day, later in her pregnancy her stomach won't be able to take all she needs in one go. At the beginning of her pregnancy the breakfast need be little more than a gesture of milk or egg, but later – into the fifth and sixth weeks – it may become as large a meal as the other. Unfortunately, as I mentioned earlier, some people-directed cats – and this includes a sizeable proportion of Orientals – absolutely refuse milk and are often uninterested in any other sort of breakfast that is 'good' for them. These may be encouraged to eat properly by offering a wedge of scrambled egg or cheese omelette – if the owner can rise to such occasions in the morning. Some cats adore a breakfast of tinned baby food. Others acquire quite a taste for one or the other of the several good makes of dried foods. Some of these are completely balanced and have constituted the sole diet of several generations of laboratory cats. Although that may sound cruel to some animal lovers cats don't mind monotony in their diet, provided, of course, they're not continually exposed to passing temptations. Cats are not stupid, particularly when they think they can better themselves. Wisely they'll refuse fish meal biscuits if they think that fifteen minutes and forty heartrending miaows later they'll be placated with poached salmon. So the way to encourage Simpering Simone to a healthy diet throughout pregnancy is to get her into the habit by presenting her with delicacies that she can't possibly refuse. When she's hooked on the idea give her a properly balanced biscuit or meal breakfast and let her get on with it. If she refuses don't give in. Pick it up. If it's been mixed with water, milk, or gravy throw it away. If it's dry put it away. Repeat the procedure next morning.

Need I remind you that every cat is a law unto itself? Some will not feel the need for breakfast until well into the fifth week of pregnancy. Some may take breakfast, a good-sized saucer of milk at lunchtime, a good dinner, and a supper-snack of whatever is going. Remember, however, that meat on its own is not enough. You must provide added minerals and vitamins. If the cat simply will not eat a varied diet including milk or bonemeal or its tablets you may have to arrange visits to the veterinarian for injections of these essential materials.

The foregoing outline on diet is just that. It's neither a bible nor an unalterable guide. Many successful breeders and average pet owners have evolved their own systems. Some are very complicated with individual menus for each day of the week and for each week of pregnancy. Some make or buy a balanced mixture which they feed at every meal throughout the entire period. The essence of their success – no matter which method they choose – is in using a variety of basic foodstuffs. Problems arise most often among those cats whose diet consists of the same single foodstuff.

That single item may be as rare as tender tongue of polar bear or as expensive as blackmail, but it alone cannot possibly provide a balanced diet. The cat may have been getting along for months without any apparent illness but the added strain of pregnancy will soon show the inadequacy of such a practice. The mother and her unborn kittens will suffer. Many owners rationalize by claiming that their cats simply will not eat anything except '———'. At one expensive boarding cattery I know the owner writes in a detailed list of his cats' likes and dislikes. This list is carefully filed. All the cats are fed exactly the same. The first day few of them eat, the second day most of them eat and by the third day even the choosiest boarder decides to accept whatever is offered. So harden your heart and plug your ears – and put down what's good for her.

How much to feed? As mentioned earlier the average adult cat gets along on about half an ounce of food for each pound it weighs. A cat who lives outdoors and must hunt and fight to live may need three or four times that amount. A cat who rises from the heat only to eat will soon become grossly overweight unless its intake is severely limited. A large well-boned tabby carrying a litter of eight may easily consume a pound of food (in two meals) during the latter stages of pregnancy. Her half-Siamese cousin twice removed and half the size may get through only six ounces. The best rule of thumb for the initiate is feed what the cat will comfortably eat within a reasonable period of say ten minutes; or whatever is normal for the cat. If she eats the lot in a gulp and looks for more you're not feeding enough. If she eats half of it and walks away you're feeding too much. Remember though that cats are competitive creatures. If they're surrounded by other cats or dogs or even curious babies they'll usually eat more quickly and more. One may trade on it. A gluttonous cat may refine her ways if she's allowed solitude in which to eat. A choosey cat may be stimulated by hungry company.

Cats are not like people. They don't suddenly decide during an early stage of pregnancy that they must walk instead of run. The normal healthy cat keeps at all her normal activities right up to the final stages of pregnancy. This may be one of the reasons why so few cats need medical or surgical help during labour. Throughout her nine weeks and a fraction she will stretch and jump and explore as before. Anxious owners who try to restrict activity may have more trouble than those who don't. It may be that this sort of over-solicitous person transfers her own fears to the cat. (Certainly, in my limited experience, highly nervous cats are often accompanied by neurotic owners.) Or it may be that normal exercise is necessary for healthy uterine tone.

The puzzling contradiction is that many cats – including laboratory cats, quarantine cats, and boarded cats – even when allowed the freedom of a large room will sit for days or weeks hardly moving from a secure corner. And they seem to have little difficulty in giving normal birth. Maybe, as some people suspect, the truth of the cat's fitness lies in the way it stretches. During the simple act of rising the cat appears to flex and extend each muscle in its body. I tried it once and almost dislocated my spine.

Another reason why most cats manage pregnancy, labour, and nursing with ease may be that their well-designed bodies haven't been drastically altered by man. Compare the cat with other domesticated creatures! Dairy cows often need emergency injections of calcium to replace that lost in their abnormally huge output of milk. The condition from which they suffer is called 'milk fever'. Without treatment the cow becomes paralysed and dies in a few hours. It is such a common ailment that every dairy farmer has seen it. Some have seen it so many times that they've learned to treat it themselves, and call the veterinary surgeon only for complicated cases. The cat too can suffer from a similar condition, but it's relatively rare. In the cat it's called calcium eclampsia or tetany. Its symptoms include a high temperature, nervousness, spasms, fits, and paralysis. If it's recognized and treated in the early stages the cat responds dramatically. Within minutes of the calcium injection the symptoms are reversed.

Overfat beef cows may suffer exactly the opposite condition. They produce no milk or too little to raise their calves. Sometimes a hormone injection or two will help them 'drop' their milk. One sees the condition in cats too, but very rarely. The treatment is the same as for the cow.

The majority of kittens are born without human assistance. Even the most coddled queen will often proudly wake her owners in the morning with an accomplished litter. Contrast that with lambing time on the farm, when without a constant night-and-day vigil many lambs are lost.

The modern sow is such a cumbersome and irksome creature that her pen must be provided with guard rails behind which the piglets gather. Without these rails piglets would be crushed as their clumsy mother turned. Infectious diseases too still cause an embarrassingly high number of deaths among piglets.

Compare the cat to its household mate. Many breeds of dog have been so altered by man that Caesarean operations are commonplace. In fact they suffer so commonly from the whole range of obstetrical troubles that some insurance rates for breeding bitches are based on the premise that one in four will require veterinary assistance. This ratio is, of course, drastically biased because quite obviously the owners of 'problem' breeds are more likely to seek insurance coverage. Nevertheless it indicates that somewhere along the line man has made a mess of the dog.

Probably the only domesticated creature which can compare to the cat in terms of health and vitality is the goat!

But despite the fact that the cat approaches perfection accidents and errors do occur. Although they occur more rarely in the cat than in other man-bound creatures we should recognize their existence and prepare. A catalogue of misfortunes and illness tends to depress some people, but early recognition can alleviate suffering.

Sadly a few cats (a very few) abort or miscarry. This may be due to an accident, to an illness, or for no apparent reason.

Despite its ability to usually land on its feet and despite its resilience the pregnant cat may suffer an abdominal injury during a bad fall. Cars can inflict as much damage on a cat as they do on us. Sadistic children and some apparently grown men have been known to kick a cat for no better reason than the fact that cats don't kick back. Whatever the cause, the injured creature may lose its kittens. A cat that comes down with a nasty flu or a nastier enteritis may also miscarry.

If the miscarriage occurs in early pregnancy the cat may show little sign of discomfort. The tiny embryos may be expelled without effort. We have no reason to suppose, however, that a miscarriage later in pregnancy isn't as traumatic for the cat as it is for the female of any other species. The expulsion of one or several large foetuses can seriously debilitate the cat. It is surely less than humane not to seek professional attention. The veterinarian will ensure that all the dead foetuses are expelled and that no infection remains. Sometimes it may be necessary to remove the entire uterus in order to save the life of the cat.

Sometimes the dead foetuses are not expelled. They remain – as foreign objects – within the uterus. If they are small they may gradually be reabsorbed by the body. If they are too large to be easily absorbed by the mother's body they begin to rot. The uterus may wall off the dead foetuses or it may attempt to expel the nasty mess. Surprisingly some cats seem to go through this without any apparent discomfort or pain. They don't miss a meal or a mouse. Quite often the condition is only discovered by the veterinarian when he examines the cat. The owners may have brought her in because 'she never seems to come on heat', or 'her kittens are weeks overdue', or 'she seems to be always on heat', or 'she seems to be getting an enormous stomach but she hasn't been out of the house for months so it couldn't possibly be kittens'. Usually the swollen uterus can be felt. Sometimes the veterinarian will want X-rays, blood tests, or a period of observation in the hospital. Almost always the only treatment is the surgical removal of the uterus and ovaries.

If a cat is mated successfully and then comes into heat a

few weeks later, repeats the process, and then does it again, you may safely assume one of two things. Either the matings aren't successful (in which case you should try another tom) or she's losing kittens when they're very young. Sometimes a regime of enforced rest and a series of hormone injections are all that's required to put her on the road to normal motherhood. More often, and this is particularly true of some highly valued but wrongly inbred queens, one must conclude with nature that her boundaries of normality have been violated. These queens should be spayed. Promulgating the line with artificial aids can only compound the problem.

Some strictly confined queens confound their owners by swelling up or making milk or cuddling objects as if they were kittens. They may become morose and disinclined to eat or neurotic and aggressive. Everyone is puzzled how she could have found her way to a tom or he to her. The explanation may be that the cat only thinks she's having kittens. The condition is called pseudo or false pregnancy. If it appears to be causing the cat any discomfort it can easily be treated. Usually the veterinarian will inject a dose of male hormone and drescribe a few tablets of the same. Less serious cases require no treatment beyond time and patience.

What measures should one observe throughout pregnancy? Little more than an extra measure of common sense. Although cats are good travellers it's not a good idea to ship them any distance, particularly during the last fortnight of pregnancy. Nor is it advisable to move them from familiar surroundings during that period.

Cat shows can be upsetting for any cat. They're subjected to the stares and prodding fingers of strangers; they're threatened by the hisses of other competitors; they're upset by the confusing smells; and not least, they're exposed to possible infection. Even the best managed and most carefully vetted shows are sometimes followed by a spate of widely disseminated disease. This may result in little more than a bit of inconvenience for the ordinary cat and its owner, but it may be disastrous for the pregnant cat. Similarly one should avoid the possibility of introducing disease into the home by refusing cat visitors, whether strays, guests, or gifts. I know an owner of two distinguished queens who purchased a superb weanling kitten while one queen was pregnant and the other was nursing six kittens. As it appeared to be in blooming health she didn't think about isolation. Unfortunately it turned out to be incubating a particularly virulent flu. The nursing kittens contracted the disease and despite treatment three died. The pregnant queen lost her kittens. And the survivors were left with a snuffly rhinitis which they didn't shake till the following summer.

Baskets and other objects may carry disease. Don't lend or borrow. Stay selfish, independent, and trouble free.

Some normally placid cats become increasingly aggressive through pregnancy. Better to warn the children that pussy doesn't want to play and remind them that those claws are for real. Not only children need beware. Other cats soon learn that the expectant mother would sooner spit than talk. Playful growing kittens usually emerge with damaged dignity from even the briefest encounter with the impatient creature. And if they're not quick to withdraw, their skin will suffer as well. Some people assert that this is all nonsense. 'Our cat would mother a baby bull if we let her,' they say. That may well be – but as a rule only after she has actually started labour or is making milk does she become receptive to strange youngsters.

Don't lightly undertake the medication of a pregnant cat! A simple worm pill has been known to cause a miscarriage. Any drug that may induce vomiting should be avoided. Many veterinarians are very cautious in the use of drugs like cortisone, streptomycin, neomycin, and chloromycetin in the ordinary cat. They may cause adverse side effects. In the pregnant cat they are best avoided altogether. Cats may react strangely to pain-killing drugs. Some have been known to go quite mad when given a tranquillizer. The best rule is not to give any drugs to a pregnant queen unless specifically instructed by your veterinarian. You may, of course, deflea a pregnant cat or rid her ears of mites, but here the rule is to make sure that all traces of the drug are removed before releasing the cat. Otherwise she may lick the stuff off and make herself ill.

Isn't it all too depressing for words? Not at all! To know the worst can only add to one's appreciation of the best. The cat (splendid creature that she is) asks for but a little extra to help her through her pregnancy. She wants a little extra food and a little extra in the way of vitamins and minerals and just a little bit of extra thought to her care. Right up to the last day of her pregnancy she'll still be prepared to share any hours you wish to spend with her. Hedonist that she is, she cannot help but teach how easy life can be. One simply watches her absorb whatever pleasures are to hand. Fires are to lie by. Shafts of sunlight are to cavort in. Passing cars are to watch. Flies are to catch. Wool is to roll in. Tweeds are to scratch on. Empty spaces are to run through. Trees are to climb. Ledges are for jumping at. Grass is to creep through. Sofas are for hide and seek. Pens are for knocking off tables. So are pencils. Life is to enjoy and new lives within are to enjoy more. How many kittens will there be? One or a dozen? Your guess is as good as mine, but I'll settle for just an average four.

2 The Cat in Labour

The feral cat seeks security from marauders and freedom from draughts, to have her kittens in seclusion. Many cats that love and trust their people will act the same; as soon as they feel the first twinge of impending kittens they search for a forgotten corner. The corner may be as simple as an unused cupboard, as maddening as 'somewhere' under the floorboards, or as inaccessible as the recesses under the furnace. Middle-aged people living in homes they've known since childhood have been led by kittening cats into unsuspected hideaways. It can be an unnerving experience if one belongs to a family that has been careless with its skeletons.

Some cats compromise. They grudgingly decide that what's good enough for people is good enough for them, and have their kittens in bed – *your* bed. This sort of cat is usually affectionate and dependent. If it's her first litter she's probably frightened as well. She needs human company and re-assurance. Later she'll want to proudly exhibit her progeny at every opportunity.

I remember a phone call I received one midnight. 'The cat has just had kittens all over the silk bedspread!' wailed

Madame hysterically. I'm never at my best on being woken up. After ascertaining that that was all she had phoned to say, I made various suggestions as to what she could do with the bedspread.

The point is that the bearing of young is not a tidy business. The cat, being a small creature, makes it a small mess, but it's a mess all the same . . . so in providing this sort of mother cat with a birthing place that is convenient for both of you you will be protecting your own interests as well as hers.

The cat that seeks seclusion usually resents any sort of handling or interference. She may scratch the hand that tries to help her. In her blind fear and aggression she may not be able to restrain herself from destroying her own young.

It's not possible to forecast with certainty how a cat will behave during kittening. One should consider her type, background, and previous behaviour. A cat that has had no human contact beyond a kick or a saucer of milk at the back door is unlikely to become dependent and solicitous. She will probably be wary and resentful, and she will certainly choose to have her kittens in a hidden spot. At the other extreme is the cat that has been used to the touch of a kind hand since birth. She demands attention and gets it. She knows that if she demands food it will be forthcoming. She'll probably choose your bed.

Some cats want it both ways. They choose a quiet dark hideaway, but they welcome a friendly human presence. Some will allow their particular favourite human to stand by, but become aggressive towards anyone else.

This conjecture about the probable or possible behaviour of a cat must appear frivolous or silly to those who believe that cats have always managed on their own. Admittedly most cats manage quite nicely; but some do not. Those of us who have accepted a cat should consider the humane principle that she's just as much ours when she's wrong as when she's right. She may have been acquired simply for the pleasure she bestows by her presence. She may have been acquired (like the majority of warehouse and farm cats) for her usefulness. She may have been brought into the home by one of the children, and allowed to stay because all of them agreed (for once in their lives) that she must.

Whatever the reason for getting the creature – and a lot of people cannot recall it – it doesn't alter the fact that she becomes your responsibility. It is cruel in the extreme (and punishable by law in many countries) to neglect her, which includes not making proper provisions for her kittening.

These provisions need be neither elaborate nor expensive. You simply have to ensure a warm quiet place which a person can get to but other animals cannot. In the case of farm or warehouse cats it's usually no problem to find an unused garage, granary, or storage area with a door. In the winter you hook up an infra-red heater. You provide water, food, a dirt corner or a litter tray, and some straw or old blankets for bedding. You visit twice a day to feed and water and see that everything is all right – you enter carefully lest she runs out – and on leaving you lock the door.

In the case of household pets you should decide well in advance which room or area of the house is going to be the cat nursery. Some people find it simplest to clear out the largest cupboard in the house. Some decide to box off a large corner of the garage, the basement, or even one of the proper people rooms. Some thoughtful owners buy or build a nesting box, which is simply a box about two feet square by two feet high with a window-cum-door in one side and a lid on the top. Many have a small heater unit in the roof.

A lid is desirable because it cuts down draughts, and provides privacy and a feeling of security. It also prevents the mother from scrambling back and forth and possibly thereby injuring her mammary glands, and later when the kittens are at the climbing stage it allows one to confine them at one's convenience. The best lining is disposable natural silk but until Wall Street recovers, one can make do with newspapers. Shavings and sawdust are dangerous materials. If eaten, they may cause an obstruction and if they go up the nasal cavities or down into the lungs, they don't do a great deal of good. Then, too, they seem to get stuck around the anus. Hay and straw facilitates fleas. Newspapers are cheap, easily available, convenient, and warm, and they do the job. Cellulose tissues are better, but they are expensive.

The nesting box can be placed in any part of the house. Often the kitchen is the most convenient. (Those who keep Siamese often find that their cats will accept a kittening box but only if it's placed in the master bedroom.) Whatever system or room you use, it is important to get the cat used to a litter tray well before the expected advent of the kittens. If the mother-to-be learned about litter trays as a kitten she'll pick up the habit again within hours. Other cats may hold themselves beyond the point of discomfort – sometimes as long as two days – before relieving themselves indoors. These may be encouraged by placing clean earth in the tray rather than the more usual newspaper, peat, or commercial litter. If the cat chooses a corner rather than the tray she must not be punished. She'll be more distressed by her lapse than even the fussiest owner. The corner should be cleaned and the tray moved to the spot. Sometimes a cat will use the litter tray and then a few moments or an hour later make a mess somewhere else. She's not out to annoy. She simply doesn't like using a dirty toilet. The solution is to either check the tray several times a day or to provide two or three of them. The latter is simple and sensible provided there's adequate space in the kittening area.

One should go to a fair bit of effort to get the litter tray system established before kittening, because otherwise the cat will be desperate to get out to her usual toilet area. Once she is used to a tray she can more easily be confined to the chosen area. And as long as she's confined she can come to no harm from outsiders, nor can she hide away from help should it be needed.

The necessity for confining the cat, or at least in restricting her to a certain area, doesn't occur to many cat owners until it's too late. Afterwards they admit that had they given it any thought they would have realized how important it is. Some experienced animal welfare workers suggest that over 90 per cent of all kittening problems could be avoided if the cat were in a restricted but accessible area. The suffering of the inexperienced and often immature cat that disappears during the latter stages of pregnancy – and appears a week later with a decomposing kitten dragging from her innards – must be blamed directly on the thoughtless owner who let her out. I could catalogue a long list of similar mishaps. Sufficient to say that as the cat gets closer to term she becomes more awkward. She may not be able to elude attackers with the same ease as formerly. She may, particularly if she's about to go into labour, become confused between her loyalty and faith in people and her instinctive urge for isolation. In short, she may find herself too far from home just when everything is about to happen.

Let's assume that the area has been chosen, and the cat has reconciled herself to living indoors. How does she indicate that she's coming close to term? She'll become restless. She may surprise herself by making some apparently uncontrollable movements, such as restless wandering, or circling or searching. She may pause in the middle of some normal activity and commence to lick herself furiously. She may nuzzle her own abdomen for moments at a time, half curious and half puzzled by its unfamiliar pressures. She may miaow the place into echoing shrieks one moment and hide in a corner the next. She may decide that she wants to be fondled continually. Quite commonly she'll break off whatever she's doing and rush to the litter tray. Then after squatting for a second she'll look up in puzzlement, give a half-hearted scratch at the litter, and move away. She may decide to shred whatever is to hand into a mattress of tiny bits. This can include anything from newspapers to your latest mink coat.

These activities, which vary from mere restlessness to seemingly neurotic outbursts to purposeful movements, are manifestations of labour, and are distinguished by the description 'first stage'. First-stage labour may be so brief or transient as to be unnoticed by the owner, or it may last as long as twenty-four hours. Aside from comforting the creature if she requests it, one can do little except provide her with food and keep a wary eye for developments. On no account should a cat be let out at this time.

Some cats refuse food. Others demand it in no uncertain manner. If she does you should provide small meals of a relatively laxative type. Cereal and milk, flaked fish with brown bread, or a bit of raw liver with commercial cat biscuit are satisfying but not constipating.

If your cat should vomit, it may mean she's eaten too large a meal. It may be reflex vomiting caused by excitement or it may be that the waves of contraction which initiate in the uterus disturb the normal digestion and set up counter peristaltic waves. Don't worry about it overmuch unless the cat continues vomiting until she is bringing up bile-stained fluid, in which case a tranquillizer may have to be administered.

Generally speaking the average or ordinary cat (if there is such a creature) has a very easy time during first-stage labour. She does a bit of wandering and tries to find a quiet corner where she can be alone. She may go through the motions of bed-making or if the materials are at hand rearrange them to her liking. Later on she begins to pant. This may alarm untutored owners. By the time they've got the veterinarian out of bed and he's explained that it's perfectly normal the cat has usually progressed to the next stage.

Some cats, Orientals and Siamese particularly, may become almost hysterical during first-stage labour. They follow the owner crying as if to summon help from the spirits. They can get themselves so worked up that they don't progress into the next stage of labour. They just keep crying and panting. Often these cats can only be helped by a tranquillizer. Unfortunately the sort of cat that can work itself into such a state of frenzied apprehension is usually the sort of cat that is difficult to medicate. Some of them, even when they're feeling benign, require six gloved hands to administer one small pill. When they're not feeling kind they'll ignore the gloves and go for your eyes. The only answer with such a cat is to bundle her into a basket and take her to the veterinarian's. (Let him protect himself as best he can. That's what he's paid for, poor devil.) If you can't pick her up and put her in a basket you must clap the open basket over her, slide a wide board under it, turn it over and close the lid as you withdraw the board.

The veterinarian will give an injection of tranquillizer and a few moments later she'll have lost the edge of her hysteria. If all goes well her body will relax sufficiently for normal labour to progress.

Fortunately this sort of cat and this sort of occurrence are rare. One tends, however, to remember the complications and to take for granted the rather marvellous fact that most cats too take it all for granted.

The second stage of labour begins with straining. One can actually see the cat contract her muscles and put all her strength into pushing the kittens into the world. At this time her hindquarters have relaxed, the vaginal orifice has enlarged, and the passage has been lubricated with a moist film. As she contracts her abdominal muscles and squeezes, the first kitten is pushed down the uterus towards the enlarged opening. The cat may strain for a moment or two, relax for a slightly longer period, and then start again. As she appears to be able to control these contractions they are termed 'voluntary'. People who have observed the birth of many kittens say that the cat appears to be in no pain during this straining, and that between bouts she appears to relax completely.

How long does it take from the time she begins straining until the whole kitten emerges? Usually from about three or four minutes up to about ten, but it's not unusual for each delivery to take as long as half an hour. Many people become very concerned after watching a favourite pet strain for fifteen minutes. After twenty minutes they've poured themselves a second stiff gin, and after thirty minutes they're unable to focus properly on the kitten as it slides into the world. That's as good a method of coping with the situation as any. The point is that you can do nothing to help the cat. You can neither ease the straining nor hasten the delivery. Best to leave her alone to get on with it in her own time – provided it's all proceeding normally. Some cats – usually Orientals – do appreciate a trusted human friend standing by. In the periods of quiescence between straining they appear to be comforted by a soft familiar voice and a tender stroke. Most, however, are intent on the procedure and are best not interrupted. Later

I'll describe the times when human assistance is not only helpful but absolutely essential.

The second stage of labour is completed by the birth of the kitten. Sometimes it emerges enveloped in a sac of membranes, sometimes with shreds of membranous tissue adhering closely to its body. In either case it's still attached by a cord of tissue to its mother. The mother immediately begins to lick the kitten. She removes (and usually swallows) all that surrounds it. During this licking she finds the umbilical cord and severs it easily. Although the cord contains the blood vessels (through which the kitten received its requirements while in the womb) it hardly bleeds when severed. Within minutes it shrivels and requires no attention other than the mother's cleansing. After a few seconds of vigorous licking the kitten is dry. But before that, even as it emerged, its mouth is already engaged in reflex movements not unlike those of a drowning man gasping for air. As the mother clears the material from around its head and from its mouth, the gasping becomes stronger and the kitten takes its first breath. For a moment or so the gasping is irregular. The chest or the abdomen may appear to contract spasmodically and without rhythm. The first few breaths may appear painful or laboured. But the will for life is as strong as the tides. Again the mouth opens and the struggle recommences. In a few seconds the gasps relax into a regular pattern. The kitten is breathing rhythmically. It opens its mouth a little wider. A sound emerges. It is half squeak and half cry. It says, 'I'm born! I'm alive! Listen to me! I'm here! I'm lost and I'm frightened, but I'm alive!' Some say that this cry of life can only be likened to a chorus of trumpets.

The miracle that is birth is not yet over. The mother must still cleanse herself of the remainder of the foetal membranes. Of these there are three. The inner layer comes away with the kitten. The middle and outer layers may come away at the same time or they may pull away easily as the mother tries to follow the end of the umbilical cord down to its root inside her own uterus. Sometimes they remain behind. They may be held up until straining begins again. And sometimes the birth of another kitten supervenes and then two separate sets of membranes come out together. This expulsion of the foetal membranes is called the third stage of labour. Its completion in the normal cat is instinctive. She casually swallows the lot. Some say that nature has decreed this action because the membranes are highly nutritious; others say it's because of their laxative effect. Some sensitive people have been known to blanch as they watch this afterbirth snack. None have reported the cat appeared to suffer in the slightest. There are, of course, contrary cats that don't eat their afterbirths. Their fastidiousness, if that's what it is, doesn't appear to have any adverse effect.

The completion of the birth of the first kitten is followed by a respite, which may be as short as five minutes but is usually ten or fifteen minutes and may be as long as an hour. The mother occupies herself with the newborn creature. She licks it, she cradles it towards her swollen nipples, and if it's able she gives it suck. And betimes she may nod her head in an approximation of a cat nap.

After the interval the mother again begins her voluntary contractions. The process is repeated exactly as for the first kitten. Two legs emerge easily. Then after a strong and protracted strain, sometimes accompanied by a cry, a groan, or a scream, the head comes through. A slight respite and then the straining begins again, and the rest of the body follows with apparent ease. And it seems that the straining has hardly eased before the mother begins her concentrated cleansing of the emerging kitten. Suddenly another lumpful of stirring cries joins the first.

Those cries are ignored by the mother while she's actually straining in labour. The newborn kittens blindly grope towards the maternal warmth. The heavy heads sway like drunken radar receivers, their inco-ordinate limbs drag forward and sideways, and their bodies roll helplessly as they cry for heat and milk. They may grope in the wrong direction. In their blind search they may find themselves trapped in a chilly impasse. It doesn't take many moments of draught or chill to rob an emergent life of its spark. That's another reason why it's important to provide a restricted area for kittening time, or a large draught-free space with uniform heat. Usually, however, even under adverse conditions the kittens manage to cradle themselves in their mother's warmth. They remain there suckling, crying, or sleeping, oblivious of her continuing labours. When she moves, as she must, somehow they cling to her side.

The third kitten, if there is a third, emerges like the others. The tiring mother may find herself having to make more of a conscious effort to expel it, but the passage is usually made easier by those that have gone before. The kitten may come head first or it may come the other way round, for both ways are normal for the cat. Some studies show that the ratio is near enough fifty-fifty. No one suggests that either is easier or more advantageous for the cat.

After giving birth to three or four kittens (over a period of anything from half an hour up to three or four) the cat may stop. She carries on as if she had completed her labours although she is obviously still carrying kittens. She eats, she nurses and cleans those that have been born, and between times she rests and relaxes in complete contentment. This interrupted labour is a perfectly normal phenomenon. After an interval of anything from half a day up to twenty-four hours she begins straining again (second-stage labour) and delivers the rest of the kittens. No one understands why this happens. We do know that it doesn't have any ill effects on the mother or the kittens. No treatment is necessary. Provided she is eating and appears well and contented, leave her alone. This is a time when mother really does know best.

A mother cat may give birth to but a single kitten. She may have a dozen or very rarely even more. The average is about four. With larger litters you should seek veterinary advice about how many she should be allowed to rear. You must accept that large litters of six or more can seriously debilitate the mother, and result in stunted weanlings. You must also remember, sad though it is, that there are far more cats in the world than there are suitable homes. Those of us who have dealt with cats in a professional capacity, as veterinarians or as animal welfare workers or both, know as an indisputable fact that a sizable minority of cats would have been better off killed at birth. The criterion must be that one allows the number that the mother cat can easily rear, and for which good homes are available. The rest should be removed as soon as possible. They should be taken to the veterinarian who will kill them with an injection. The only pain is the prick of the needle. Drowning or gassing a kitten, however young, is cruel.

I know that that's a sad and sorry jolt to inject into a description of the miracle of birth – but Nature doesn't content herself with being beautiful. She can be cruel. The prolific cat produces many kittens because many do not survive the rigours of an unprotected existence. Let us rear only those which we can protect. Then we can peacefully watch the mother cat with her kittens. We can cherish them as she does. We can share her contentment as one by one their cries are stilled as they find the nipple. They drink. Finally, satisfied, they drop their heads in sleep. They need it. It's a bit tiring, this business of being born.

3 The Cat in Trouble

Obviously it is much better to help the cat, if she is going to need help, before she has used up her vital store of strength. A minor problem can develop into a major crisis in just a few hours, and sometimes just a few minutes.

What are the possible problems and how does one cope with them?

One of the most common causes of panic phone calls is a cat that produces a bit of a kitten and then gives up. If the situation is only a few moments old, it's usually best to wait a few more short minutes before taking any action, provided that she appears perfectly comfortable. If she's obviously uncomfortable or appears unable to complete the act, then you must help her. (I am assuming, of course, that you can't get hold of your veterinarian, or that you're acting under his instructions.) Have someone hold the cat around her shoulders, gently but firmly. Lay out a smallish clean towel or rough cloth, say about a foot square. Then wash your hands thoroughly. If you have some Dettol or some equally safe antiseptic, mix some in a bowl and wash with that. Then examine the emerging kitten. You're looking for only one reason – to make sure that both the emerging legs are from the same end of the kitten. If they are not you should get the cat to a veterinarian if at all possible. He may tie a piece of bandage to one of the protruding legs only and then shove the kitten back into the cavity, and wait for the mother to start contracting again. If the female cat is tractable, he may insert a scrubbed and sterilized index finger into the vagina and try to straighten the kitten. The younger veterinarians in my practice, I note, are much more prone to immediately stick them on the anaesthetic machine and reach for the Caesarean kit.

If the mother has worn herself out and simply hasn't the strength to strain you may have to exert a fair bit more pressure to pull the kitten away. There are two dangers in the procedure. The first is that you can actually tear the kitten in half, as may happen if you simply tug at its feet. It cannot happen if you keep the towel flat over as much of the kitten as possible and exert even pressure over the whole surface of its body.

The second danger is that you may injure the mother. This can happen if the kitten is over-large or wedged in at the wrong angle, or if the secretions are all dried up. If the kitten appears of average size, try to adjust it by pushing it back about half an inch or an inch and then rotating it slightly. Then pull gently with short side-to-side tugs rather than one straight jerk. If the kitten is very dry, cover it with mineral oil or a similar lubricant, then push it partway back in and give it a further gentle try.

Those instructions may appear difficult if not impossible when viewed coldly on paper. Many people swear by all their sensitivities that they could never bring themselves to do such a thing, but when they are actually faced with the situation they somehow find reserves and capabilities within themselves they never suspected. On countless occasions I have relayed just such instructions over the telephone, prefacing them with an injunction to keep calm because the worst that could happen would be that the task would prove to be too difficult and the cat would have to be bundled into a basket and brought along to the surgery. Usually I ask the owners not to hang up but to keep the line open and inform me of their progress. In the majority of cases the whole procedure from panic phone call to relieved thank-you's takes less than ten minutes. In some cases the kitten proves to be too large or malformed or the pelvis of the mother (due to previous injury) is not normal. You can do no harm, however, by giving a gentle try. Emphasis on the word *gentle*, please! Countless kittens have been saved by this simple first-aid, and I've yet to hear of a case where the mother was injured provided the owner remained calm and followed the dictates of common sense.

After such a delivery the mother may rest for as long as four or five hours. Some, however, will immediately start straining and produce the subsequent kittens without apparent difficulty. Others will be so weak that they appear to completely give up. Although they've obviously got more unborn kittens they simply can't or won't make any further effort.

How do you judge the situation? Each case of course is slightly different (which is what makes veterinary medicine and animal husbandry an art as well as a science). If, for example, one has successfully delivered the recalcitrant kitten and within minutes the mother has cleansed it and it is resting quite happily by her side and she herself appears contented and resting, the thing to do is nothing. Leave her alone to rest. Check every half hour or so to see that she is still resting and requires no further assistance. If it's two o'clock in the morning it's best to go back to sleep and set the alarm for at least two checkups during the night.

If on the other hand the mother appears uncomfortable, and is unable to either sleep or nurse the kitten properly, it's better to get her to the veterinarian.

Between these two obvious extremes lie a score of gradations. One factor that is far more important than most people admit is the time of day or night. Most veterinary establishments are fully staffed by day and fitfully asleep by night. No patient gets the best possible treatment at night. That should be patently obvious. Amazing then how many people will watch their cat become progressively weaker during the day and into the evening while they attempt to feed it glucose water and encourage it by making clucking noises. Then as the world goes to sleep and even the television gets bored with itself they decide that what the cat really needs is a veterinarian and she needs it now. Why on earth such people don't have the brains and the consideration to at least ring for advice during the early stages one cannot imagine. No veterinarian minds a call during the day to report progress. I know few who don't resent being called at two o'clock in the morning to attend a condition that has been brewing all the previous day.

Forgive the irritable intrusion. Let's get back to the first-aid. Another very common problem is the kitten that for a variety of reasons needs human help to start breathing. Sometimes the mother fails to remove the fetal membranes. The kitten lies in its sac feebly gasping, literally drowning in its own juices. Sometimes the mother has removed the sac partially but the kitten's mouth is still enveloped. And sometimes, although there seems to be no reason, the kitten just doesn't give that spirited effort needed to initiate those first vital gasps.

Again the only materials needed are a few strips of clean towel or thick cloth (thick but soft paper towels are admirable for the purpose) and a pair of clean hands. The membranes are easily removed by simply grasping them with a dry towel and peeling them off. If the membranes are intact and adhering tightly to the kitten they may have to be torn. Usually a pinch between two fingernails is sufficient. Use another piece to wipe off those bits adherent to the mouth and nose and yet another bit to dry the tiny mouth. If the mouth is full of fluid some experienced breeders and veterinarians say that the best method to get rid of it is to suspend the kitten by its hind legs and swing it slowly back and forth three or four times the full arc of your outstretched arm. This will not only expel the fluid from the mouth but will release a far greater volume which obviously must have been contained in the abdomen. For that reason it appears to confer psychological benefit on the operator, and has become a very popular method in many veterinary establishments and breeding catteries.

Whether the benefits are real or apparent I do not know but many kittens start to breathe after a swinging session.

Some experienced hands prefer to limit their efforts to a gentle drying of the mouth followed by a vigorous rub of the kitten's whole body with a towel. The procedure looks not unlike an angry housewife showing a maid how a glass is really meant to be polished. Initiates seeing this towel massage for the first time predictably exclaim that such rough handling must hurt the kitten.

During this initial massage-and-dry-up the kitten usually starts to breathe on its own. Then all you need do is place it in a warm box until the mother is ready to accept it. Some kittens need more help. One method of artificial respiration is to press down gently but firmly, and then release; down and on its side with its head extended forward and slightly lower than the rest of the body. Place the palm flat over its chest, press down gently but firmly, and then release; down and release, at the rate of about ten or less a minute. (You need hardly any pressure at all.)

Some people prefer mouth-to-mouth resuscitation. You can easily surround the whole muzzle including the nostrils of the kitten. Breathe in and out – about ten to the minute. Don't use too much strength or take very deep breaths. The main danger is that you may blow some fluid back into the lungs, so inhale first and spit out the fluid. The main drawback to his method is that many people, no matter how attached they are to their animals, simply cannot bring themselves to do it. They know full well that there is less danger of picking up disease or infection from a newly born kitten than there is from a strange human who has collapsed in the street, but they cannot overcome their repugnance of the idea.

Some catteries and cat breeders find it worth while to buy or rent an oxygen cylinder and attach it with a couple of simple tubes to a closed box, which they dignify by giving it the name oxygen tent. Such a set-up need not be very expensive. Most companies charge only a nominal rent for the oxygen cylinder, and will sell you the tube and the valve that goes with it very cheaply. They then charge only for the oxygen which is actually used. As the newborn kittens are dried they are placed in the oxygen tent. The valve or flow meter can be adjusted so that there is a constant but small flow of oxygen into the box. Never aim at anything like a hundred per cent oxygen – this would be harmful. The goal is to provide just a little additional oxygen to the normal supply of air. There is no danger whatsoever in the method, provided you don't give too much oxygen.

Some people apply spirits of ammonia and other aromatic spirits to the nostrils and mouth of newborn kittens. Almost invariably these do more harm than good.

Some breeders keep quite a handsome supply of dangerous injectable drugs. These may only be given directly into the heart of the newborn kitten. As intravenous injection into a newborn kitten is a very skilled procedure, the use of these drugs in unskilled hands – and indeed in most skilled hands – almost always proves immediately fatal.

Some people advise that newborn kittens that don't breathe immediately should be dipped into pails of hot and cold water alternatively. I have yet to hear of this procedure ever saving a kitten.

The vast majority of newborn kittens breathe on their own without assistance within sixty to ninety seconds of being born. The vast majority of kittens that do not have the strength to start breathing on their own within two minutes will not breathe, no matter what vigorous efforts are made to help them.

I must point out, however, that very many kittens that have been given up by the owners and occasionally by the mother as dead are in fact very much alive, and surprise everyone a few minutes later by their hearty screams. These are, of course, screams of indignation at having been so lightly cast aside.

Now we must discuss the mystique of the umbilical cord. Every text, every book of instruction, every breeder's guide contains a long list of instruments and materials and instructions all of which are absolutely essential (so they claim) in order to successfully ligate the umbilical cord. Without this attention, they claim, the cord becomes infected, the newly born animal becomes febrile, and within days it will be dead. These admonitions and instructions must have been passed down from so-called expert to so-called expert ever since the first man assisted at the first animal birth.

It would be amusing, if not instructive, to compile a list of these directions from several different manuals on the subject. Some state very firmly that one must tie the umbilical cord no more than three inches from the body of the newborn kitten, using boiled cotton or silk. Others state that under no circumstances must one tie the umbilical cord. One places a forceps on the cord as close to the animal's body as possible and another forceps adjacent to the first, and twists. Still others advise putting the forceps close to the kitten's body and cutting the cord away from the mother with sterilized scissors. Variations on the theme seem to be limited only by the imagination of the authors.

May I be permitted to introduce a revolutionary new method! I hasten, in my modesty, to admit that this revolutionary concept is not mine. I have stolen it. I have stolen it from those who really know what they're talking about. They say that the cord is best severed by the mother cat. If for some reason she is unable to do so, it will break naturally by traction. In other words, it is quite unnecessary to interfere. Nature, so far as umbilical cords are concerned, knows exactly what she's doing. In too many cases, when man tries to lend a hand he makes a terrible mess. This is one more case where laziness wins the race and true virtue lies in sloth.

Obviously in practically all cases where the kitten remains attached to the mother by the cord it will still be partially surrounded with afterbirth. While removing the bits and rubbing the kitten the cord usually separates naturally.

Sometimes, of course, despite all one's efforts a cat decides to have her kittens in the most unsuitable location. You find her later with her litter apparently completely healthy. A day or two later you notice that the cords appear enlarged and festering. You must then apply local antiseptics. They must be applied at least three times a day and for at least five days to have any effect. Many veterinarians suggest tincture of iodine as being the most effective antiseptic for an infected navel, but some say that iodine in any form is too irritating for the kitten. Some suggest 5 per cent tannic and 5 per cent salicylic acid in 70 per cent alcohol. Some make up and dispense a formula which includes camphor, tannic acid, and alum. This is called an astringent antiseptic. Its main advantage is that it helps the stump to dry quicker, and, as we all know, in most cases the drier the tissues the faster the healing.

There is no point in doing this sloppily. You should wash the area carefully with saline (one teaspoon of salt to one pint of water, boiled and allowed to cool, kept in a sterile container), then dry, and then apply the antiseptic of choice. If on the following day the area appears redder or more inflamed or infected you must, of course, contact the veterinarian. He may decide that the condition is so bad that it requires an antibiotic. If he decides that the antibiotic will have sufficient effect applied locally, he will dispense either an antibiotic ointment or an antibiotic dusting powder. If the kitten is off its food or cries continuously, or if it's running a temperature of 103, the veterinarian will probably inaugurate a course of general antibiotic therapy; that is, that he will want the antibiotic to reach all the tissues of the kitten. Newborn kittens are rather small for injections. Newborn Siamese kittens can be very tiny indeed.

Some antibiotics, if given by injection or by mouth to the mother, will reach the milk in sufficient quantity to have a therapeutic or healing effect on the infected kitten. Another way of treating a newborn kitten with antibiotics is to smear the antibiotics in powder form mixed with honey on to the udder of the nursing mother. At least one pharmaceutical company makes an ointment which contains an antibiotic which can be given effectively and safely by mouth to newborn kittens. You don't, of course, attempt to force it into the kitten's mouth. All you need do is smear the material around the mouth. One of these products, for example, is given at the dosage rate of one half inch of ointment for each pound that the kitten weighs. As a newborn kitten weighs much less than a pound, you can readily see that it is a very simple procedure.

Sometimes a slightly sore navel will be licked into a raging infection by the kitten's mother or by one of its brothers or sisters. In these rare cases you must of course separate the infected kitten.

During the hot months you must remember that the newborn kitten is virtually helpless against many insects. One of the very pitiful sights is to see one that has become flyblown. The only cure is prevention. You must keep the area clean, screening or netting as you would for a human baby in the same circumstances.

Finally may I point out the very distressing fact that sometimes a kittening cat will turn on those already born. This cannibalism may be triggered by one of several reasons. The most common is that the mother cat has been frightened by a stranger, be it an adult or a child or another animal. The solution is obvious.

Some cats become increasingly aggressive during their pregnancy. When her newborn kittens start to cry this lowers her aggression and she begins to take care of them. Sometimes, however, their cries are not sufficient to lower her aggressive instinct and she turns on them. In those cases one must remove the kittens until the kittening time is over. When labour is completed the mother cat often becomes much quieter and will accept all her kittens.

Sometimes the mother cat turns on her newly born kittens just as they begin to nurse. Examine her carefully. She may have a sore infected teat. If only a single teat is involved sometimes the only treatment necessary is a gentle squeezing to milk off the surplus. Sometimes a soothing ointment and a bandage is required. Sometimes the teat is sore because it contains an abscess. These are extremely painful. If it appears about ready to burst, you may bathe it with warm salt water. When it opens wash it thoroughly, apply a soothing ointment, and cover with a protective bandage. Then take the cat along to the veterinarian. If an injection of antibiotics isn't given within a few hours the infection may spread to the other teats.

If the whole udder area seems to be infected or inflamed or sore, remove the kittens from the mother until kittening is completely finished. Put the kittens in one box over a hot water bottle. Put the mother cat in her basket and take the whole lot along to your veterinarian. He will probably give the mother cat a tranquillizing injection. Then he will attempt to milk out all the surplus fluid, then give an injection of antibiotic. An hour or two later he will attempt to once again introduce the kittens to the mother.

Very occasionally one meets a cat that for no discernible reason will turn on her kittens and devour them. Sometimes this happens to a maiden cat. The breeder tries her once again. The second time she proves thoroughly admirable. If, however, on the second attempt one witnesses a repetition of the slaughter that occurred on the first occasion one should not breed the cat again.

After all, there are some cats, like some people, that only learn about true happiness after they have had their ovaries and uterus removed.

POSTPARTUM HAEMORRHAGE AND OTHER POST-LABOUR COMPLICATIONS

Let me assure you that the vast majority of cases in which there is haemorrhage following parturition the haemorrhage is of such a minor nature as to be without significance. In most cases it originates in a slight bruise or a slight tear. Clotting and subsequent healing occur without human aid.

Occasionally there is a fair bit of bleeding from the ruptured end of the umbilical cord. Sometimes an assisted delivery produces a fair bit more. The blood seems to flow in a stream as the kitten is pulled away. I think I can fairly state, and I hope it is reassuring, that I have never seen a cat die from haemorrhage during or shortly after giving birth to kittens. In most cases the bleeding stops fairly quickly on its own. Sometimes it persists a bit longer but in diminishing quantities. Provided one doesn't mess about and try to insert tampons or bandages or tissues, and provided the cat is allowed to rest quietly, there is no immediate danger.

Most authorities agree that the vast majority of cases require no treatment at this time. However if the haemorrhage persists beyond a reasonable time, or if there is an extremely large flow of blood, you must of course call the veterinarian.

Depending on the source of the haemorrhage that gentleman may give an injection of adrenalin, or posterior pituitary hormone, vitamin K, or other drugs. Sometimes he may have to give the cat a whiff of anaesthetic and try to locate the ruptured blood vessel or vessels. They may be easily accessible in the vulva or they may be in the uterus, in which case an operation will be necessary.

A far more common form of postpartum haemorrhage is that which only occurs sporadically and in small amounts, but seems to go on for several days. If the amount is slight – say a drop or two up to a quarter of a teaspoonful – and only occurs when the cat strains to urinate or defecate, the cause is probably a very slight tear in the uterus or more likely the cervic or vulva. These usually clear up without any treatment.

If the amount of bleeding is greater and occurs even when the cat is not straining, the internal damage is more extensive and the cat had better be checked by a veterinarian when it is convenient. He may decide that an injection or two of antibiotic is all that's needed in order to guard against the possibility of infection in those wounds. Or if the cat has abdominal pain and a temperature he may decide to hospitalize her for further observation and possibly an operation.

A less alarming but almost invariable complication following labour is the swelling of the vulvar lips. This external sexual organ can get very bruised and sore even during a normal delivery. Fortunately in most cases the swelling goes down within a few hours without any treatment. If the cat appears bothered by it, however, and leaves off nursing her kittens in order to lick the area, you can often afford her considerable relief by applying damp cloths to the area. Fill two bowls with water, one warm (but not hot enough to burn) and the other cold with ice cubes in it. Holding a cloth in each hand, so that you can gauge their comfort, apply them alternately. After fifteen or twenty minutes the swelling is usually considerably reduced.

Sometimes the cat gets a blood blister in the vulva. The whole area is rather sensitive during labour. Any injury, whether self-inflicted, from another animal, or from an inconsiderate child, may bring on one of these rather ugly swellings. They are called haematomas. There is no point in bathing these tense blisters. If they are small and causing no urinary obstruction or other difficulty they are best left alone, and are usually absorbed within one to two weeks. If they are troublesome an appointment should be made with the veterinarian. As a rule he will not interfere for three or four days. He may then inject a drug called hyaluronidase into the blister to help absorption, or he may decide to drain it through a needle and syringe. In more serious cases he may feel that an anaesthetic and proper operation are necessary.

One of the most alarming sights following parturition is prolapse of the rectum. To the novice owner or breeder it can (understandably) be such an alarming sight that it robs them of all their carefully nurtured reserves of calm. They hysterically report that their beloved cat is turning inside out. But although that indeed may be exactly what is happening, there is decidedly a limit beyond which the inside can't come outside.

During the pains of labour it is not uncommon for the rectum to come out a distance of a quarter or a half inch. Almost always as straining ceases it will go back in on its own. Sometimes, though, two or three inches or even more are forced out, and then you must act. Warm up a pint of hot water and add a teaspoonful of salt. In that solution soak two or three soft cloths, and apply them gently to the protruding tissue. As the cloths dry and cool change them. Using very gentle pressure, ease the rectum back into position. If the cat has not finished kittening you will then have to get on the telephone to the veterinarian, because almost certainly the next time she starts straining the rectum will come out again. All that you as an owner can do is to try and get it in as soon as possible and keep it in until you get the animal to the veterinarian's. If one allows it to remain outside for some hours it may be permanently damaged and a portion may have to be amputated.

The same principles apply when the uterus is forced out during excess straining. One tries to gently ease it back in, using wet cloths. If a considerable volume of the uterus has been exposed to the elements for some time it may have been injured and it will certainly be swollen and sore. Boil up several pints of water. Add one teaspoonful of salt per pint. Allow to cool to comfortable body temperature and pour slowly and liberally over the uterus. You may have to do this for several long moments before it returns to anything like normal. Sometimes it will then gently ease back into the body. More often it will not – at least not without more expertise than the average owner has.

You have, however, stopped the destructive process of exposure and initiated the restoration of normal tone. Then, one gets on the phone and warns the veterinarian that you are on the way. Place the kittens already born in a lined box on some newspapers over a hot water bottle. If you don't take them along the mother cat, ignoring her own perilous position, will leap out of any moving car window in an attempt to rejoin them. But even with the kittens in the same car you must remember that the mother cat can easily injure herself. Wrap her in a blanket and hold her firmly. If you are on your own you're best to place the kittens in one box and the mother in a closed basket and let her take her chances. If you attempt to drive with one hand and hold her with the other, chances are that eventually she'll end up in a veterinary hospital, but you'll end up in the morgue.

One of the very rare complications following the birth of kittens is a paralysis of the hindquarters. The cat seems perfectly all right. She nurses her kittens. She eats. She remains interested in all about her. But she must pull herself about with her front legs, dragging her rear end behind. This condition is thought to be caused by damage to the nerves of the mother as an extra large kitten passes through the pelvic canal. Injections of drugs called anabolic steroids and of the B-complex vitamins help to hasten recovery, but good nursing is essential also. This includes turning the mother at half-hour intervals during the day and night so that she doesn't become sore and ulcerated, giving enemas if she can't pass her motion, and gently applying pressure over the bladder if she can't urinate. Three out of four recover without complication after about a week in the hospital.

Other forms of paralysis that occur following parturition may be due to such things as infections or toxic diseases or accidents or starvation or multiple vitamin deficiency. In these cases, however, she will show other symptoms besides paralysis. Pinpointing the cause and outlining therapy is obviously a professional matter.

A very small percentage of cats don't pass their afterbirths. The foetal membranes stay behind. The cat will be off her food and uncomfortable, and she may have a thickish brown discharge from the vagina. She will resent any handling of the abdomen, because it will be painful.

Generally these symptoms show up within three days of kittening. At that stage treatment is relatively straightforward. The veterinarian will use injections of hormones (usually stilboestrol or posterior pituitary extract) and antibiotics.

Metritis, which means an inflammation of the uterus, also occurs within three days of kittening. The symptoms are about the same as those of retained afterbirths. In addition the mother cat may be very thirsty, she may vomit, and she will take no interest in her kittens whatsoever. The earlier the treatment the better the chances of an early recovery and a return to normal nursing. Immediately on presentation of the patient the veterinarian will inaugurate a course of high-level antibiotics.

Finally I would like to go into some detail about a condition I mentioned earlier as being called milk fever, or more properly lactation tetany. Usually this condition does not occur until the cat has been nursing for at least two weeks. It may even occur when the kittens are eight weeks of age or older. However, as it can happen within a day or two of kittening, I include it here.

The mother cat becomes increasingly nervous. Her pupils may dilate, her mouth may go dry, and she may start to breathe very quickly. She sometimes staggers about and can't seem to place her feet properly. Then her muscles start to shake; she collapses; and an hour or two or three later she goes into a coma.

This alarming set of symptoms is more likely to appear in a smallish cat that is nursing a large litter. Age doesn't seem to have a great deal to do with it – cases have been reported in cats between one and six years of age. Many veterinarians in dairy practice find that a heifer or a cow that has milk fever at one calving seems to be more prone to have it at subsequent calvings. We can't make this comparison so readily among breeding cats because once a cat has had milk fever many owners wisely decide that they'd rather not take a chance on her going through it again. After she is cured and the litter is weaned they have her spayed.

Strange to relate, we don't know if diet has a great deal to do with this condition. Many cats that have been on scientifically balanced diets with adequate amounts of calcium have come down with it. Some experts say it occurs not because the cat is fed improperly, but because she herself cannot utilize what she is getting.

The essential part of the treatment is the injection of calcium solutions. The one most commonly used is calcium borogluconate. It is best given slowly and intravenously, and it is best given by a veterinarian. If it is given without caution and experienced observation one may cause heartblock and death.

Another way of giving the calcium is subcutaneously. This method however is slower, more painful, and less effective, and it may cause sloughs or abscesses. Either method gives the most fantastic results. Usually within seconds or very short minutes the cat is back to normal. You should of course reduce the number of kittens or remove them altogether, and, needless to say, if you can't be convinced that she should be spayed, on subsequent occasions she should only be allowed a normal four kittens at the outside. May I conclude by repeating that the cat is the most resilient of all the creatures that share our mundane lives! Given half a chance she will bounce back from the depths of an illness that would kill you, me, and my little dog named Henry. That half a chance need consist of no more than a modicum of common sense plus a phone call to the veterinarian.

Part III
THE KITTENS

1 The Suckling Kitten

The newly born kitten is a helpless creature. It can do little more than weave its head and propel itself a short distance. If one contrasts an hour-old kitten with a freshly born deer (or antelope or horse) one realizes how truly helpless the cat is. Any of those baby herbivores will be – granted, very unsteadily – standing within minutes. If faced with a bristling dog they will instinctively snort, paw or strike with their front legs, turn tail and make a credible display of running. They belong to species that live on the move. Those that can't move quickly enough don't survive.

The cat chooses a nest hidden from enemies. There her helpless kittens remain secure, unseen and seeing little, for many days.

During that time the mother is almost always available to give them suckle. Each kitten spends almost a quarter of its time suckling. The mother, however, spends between fifteen and eighteen hours a day being suckled. The reason is that quite often kittens will suckle individually and in succession. Though the mother initiates the nursing by nuzzling and licking she may succeed in arousing only a single kitten at a time. As it takes its fill and drops off to sleep another may wake. And so it goes. Not very efficient or scientific, perhaps, but the mother doesn't seem to mind – at least when the kittens are very young.

If you could observe a newly born litter closely without disturbing them, you would notice that they soon become very attached to a particular corner of their nest. If you remove them from this corner and put them in a strange place they often begin to cry, and will be comforted only if they are again allowed to lie by their mother or if the odour from the familiar corner is moved to the new site. That familiar odour, incidentally, is produced by the discharge of the female before, during, and after birth. The practical application of this bit of behavioural observation is that although you may remove much of the mess (provided of course that the mother isn't upset by your presence) and you must of course remove the soiled bedding, you should not scrub the cage before the kittens are five days old. It is at about then, although their eyes are not properly opened, that they begin to see their way dimly about the home corner. When they are about ten days old they can usually manage to see their way about the entire cage.

It is rather marvellous that a very young and naïve queen, with neither prior experience nor instruction, should without any apparent anxiety know exactly how to circle her kittens with her legs, cradle them towards her abdomen, and lick them vigorously to stimulate them into the only activity of which they are properly capable at that age – suckling.

At the beginning the kittens' reactions are not quite so ordered. There's a fair bit of fumbling and weaving before a nipple is finally firmly grasped. Even the most awkward kitten, however, is not slow to learn this most essential of lessons. At the end of eight or twelve hours its expertise is impressive.

At this stage the sense of smell appears to be most important. Kittens without the organs necessary for smelling can nurse relatively easily from a bottle with an artificial nipple, but cannot manage to nurse naturally.

Some breeders have observed that each kitten chooses an

individual nipple which it prefers throughout the nursing period. Some scientists think that this insistence on private ownership is Nature's way of preventing fights in which the mother's delicate mammary tissues might be injured, but I have my doubts about that theory, because it is the younger kittens, which are least capable of doing damage, that are most attached to their individual nipples. As the kitten reaches three weeks of age its ability to inflict damage is much greater, yet its attachment to an individual nipple grows less.

During the first three weeks suckling is initiated by the encouragement of the mother cat. During the third week the kittens begin to take the initiative, and after the fourth week the process increasingly becomes a case of the reluctant mother being followed about by demanding kittens.

Even the most urbanized among us, while driving through the diminishing countryside, have seen lambs and colts and calves butting their mothers' udders to start the milk flowing. The kitten too gives a certain amount of prodding when it wants to start suckling, using its front feet in a slow pummelling motion called a 'milk tread'. It is interesting to note that the kitten doesn't use this movement until it is a few days old, whereas both the rat and the hamster use it from birth.

The newly born kitten uses its paws to push the fur and skin back from the teat, thus making it easier to grasp. At that stage the milk flows sufficiently quickly, but after a few days it doesn't flow quickly enough. Then kitten encourages it along with its treading motion.

Not until the kittens are two or sometimes three weeks of age do they take a few hesitant steps away from the home nest. Within three or four days their courage (or is it curiosity?) develops apace. They may take a dozen kitten steps and four giant cat hops away from their mother before a wave of insecurity (or is it caution?) sweeps them back in one headlong tumble.

It's then that the real joys – and the real labour – of kitten sponsorship begin. Let us, however, consider again those exciting first few hours, when panics may occur and lives may be lost, and when realistic decisions must be made as to which lives will be spared and which if any must be ended.

The most common cause of death in the newborn kitten is chilling. We know not why a kitten will roll away from the warmth of its mother into a chilly pocket from which it is helpless to extricate itself and which its otherwise occupied mother appears to regard as remote as another continent. No one knows what mechanism drives a mother to care for some of her offspring while ignoring others. And once a mother cat – or sow or bitch – takes it into her head to ignore one of her litter, all the wiles of husbandry and medicine often won't succeed in changing her mind.

One thing is certain. If a cat has a litter in an unexpected place and time, and you find that place only because of the weakening cries of a chilling kitten – and if you then take that kitten and replace it by its mother while it is still wet and cold – she will treat it as an unwanted intruder, either pushing or carrying it away or killing it. I have found only one rescue method that sometimes works: Place the kitten on or near a source of heat that is so hot that you can hardly bear to hold your hand on it. (You must, of course, be careful not to burn the kitten or asphyxiate it in rising fumes.) I have heard kittens that were absolutely cold to the touch and too weak to cry, scream for their first suckle within a half hour of careful warming. If the kitten has been away from its mother for several hours, and its mother is otherwise occupied when it recovers sufficiently to be replaced, you may sustain it with the following mixture: one pint of water with two tablespoonfuls of glucose and one quarter level teaspoonful of salt, boiled and fed at body temperature.* A teaspoon given a drop at a time is adequate to sustain the kitten for a couple or three hours during which an opportune time should arise to re-present it to its mother.

The best time to attempt the introduction of a rejected kitten is just after the mother has got the others suckling. First stroke the mother. If any of her wet discharges are still about rub a bit into your hands. Then pick up two or

* The formula is a standard one which many veterinarians suggest as sensible home aid in cases in which great amounts of fluid have been lost.

three of the suckling kittens, add the rejected kitten to your handful, and replace the lot. The procedure requires a fair bit of judgement (acquired by experience) or better still just a feeling for animals. If the kittening mother doesn't know and trust you, it may be better to try and rear the rejected kitten as an orphan for the first day or two. Why? During kittening, which may be a time of confusing sensations, the mother, if wrongly pressed, may turn on *all* her newborn. You must remember that throughout the later stages of her pregnancy her instinctive aggression towards all strangers may have partially or completely blotted out many layers of her acquired trust. The alien odour or appearance of the revived kitten may trigger off an unselective aggressive fury which abates only after every living creature has been driven off or killed.

Sometimes deaths occur because the mother insists on moving her kittens from place to place. Even though she apparently never loses count, she may lose a kitten through one of the many hazards inherent in such moves. A marauding dog, a hungry rat, or unthinking children have all been known to take their toll of the untended fraction. The most dedicated mother cat cannot be in two places at one time. Sometimes before a move has been completed the former home becomes inaccessible. Under natural conditions this sudden cut-off may be caused by storms or floods or fires or great movements of the earth. Many more kittens, however, are isolated by man's barriers. Many a farm cat has been disturbed by the shifting of storage hay in a loft. If the unsuspecting labourer finishes his task and shuts off a section of the loft while she is furtively moving her family, she will be unable to complete it. Unused garages and warehouses, other favourite nesting spots, may become scenes of activity during the nursing period, and again the cat may decide to move with tragic results.

There are three basic attitudes found among nursing mother cats, the most common of which prevails in cats that have never had any reason to trust people. Such a mother wishes to rear her young in isolation. She may accept handouts at a distance, but should you attempt any familiarity with the litter she will either kill them or pick them up and be gone. There's a lesson to be learned: unless a nursing cat is known to be affectionate and trusting, you can help her best by leaving her nest alone. Only if you hear the kittens crying, in that unmistakable haunting tone that means hunger, should you investigate, cautiously, while the mother is absent. If she's a particularly young or tiny creature it might be advisable to remove all but four of the kittens. Sometimes it is apparent that the mother herself has decided to abandon one or more of the weakest kittens. It would be cruel not to aid her in that task, and hasten the impending deaths.

May I repeat? In most cases untrusting cats are best left alone throughout the entire period. Too often any interference results in a hasty move or blind massacre.

The average household pet (if there is such a creature) will accept help from known members of the human family during the kittening period and afterwards, and will tolerate a certain amount of gentle attention to the nest and nursing kittens. You may change the wet bedding and briefly examine the kittens to make sure that everything is all right. It would be courting trouble, however, to remove kittens less than three weeks old for too long a period. Needless to say strange animals should be kept away lest they trigger an outburst of anger, and children should be allowed to view only under supervision. That supervision should include a prior understanding that comments will be made quietly and stroking will be brief and gentle. (In these sensitive three weeks, the best rule is *no* stroking or touching.)

Those of us who have kept or been kept by 'average' cats can bear witness to the wide variations on the theme. Some no sooner complete the first suckling round than they must carry each kitten in its turn to the master bedroom (this always happens at five o'clock in the morning) for inspection and approbation. Some appear unable to settle down to the suckling routine unless comforted by their own mother or daughter or sister or even brother. I know one Blue Persian who is so attached to a creaky old collie that she insists he share the nest.

That so-called average group of nursing mothers contains

innumerable eccentric exceptions to the rule. The third group – cats who are almost completely orientated to humans – contains few creatures about which one can lay down *any* rules. Many Orientals fall into this third category, but so do many purebreds without foreign pretensions. So do many other cats whose pedigrees, if they were known, would shock a Parisian taxi-driver. The only qualification needed to belong to this group is to be devoted to and loved by a particular human being (or two at the most) to the exclusion of everything else.

These are the cats that tend to get hysterical and demanding during first stage labour, and that tend to have their kittens in your bed despite all precautions. These are the cats that insist that you share all the sleepless hours that the first three weeks of motherhood demand. Many cats in this group are so fastidious that if you don't change their bedding two or three or sometimes even four times a day they will move themselves, kittens, baggage, and all, into the cleanest corner of your linen closet. As the baggage may include anything from a half pound of smoked salmon to a wedge of overripe Brie, the linen closet doesn't remain suitable for long. The next move may be to the centre of a velvet-covered sofa, to the front seat of the Jaguar (borrowed from the boss) or in the pantry among the fruit cakes you volunteered to keep for the W.I. The move is never considered satisfactory unless accompanied by a rotting herring or an ancient chicken carcass. I can't tell you much else about that sort of cat because their owners tend, after a while, to phone the veterinarian less and the psychiatrist more.

The cry of an unsatisfied kitten is unmistakable. If you hear it, examine the queen, either approaching her directly, cajoling her with food, or catching her as she leaves the nest, depending on her temperament.

Examine her carefully. She may be ill. See if she has any signs of infection. Gently squeeze her nipples. Has she any milk? Most of the common problems of kittening are discussed in 'The Cat in Trouble', and most of those troubles require professional veterinary attention as soon as possible.

If the whole litter is crying in hunger, the fault generally lies in the mother.

If only one or two kittens are unhappy common sense dictates we should direct our attention to them. A kitten may be chilled and abandoned, or it may have a deformity which prevents it from suckling properly. Examine it carefully! It may have a misshapen or enlarged head or other abnormality which renders it obviously unfit to survive. Open its mouth – it may have a cleft palate. When the kitten suckles the milk goes up into the roof of its mouth and dribbles down its nose. There is an operation, not too complicated, to correct the condition; but in most cases it's advisable to have the kitten put to sleep, for several reasons. First, it is thought that the condition, or at least the tendency to the condition, is hereditary. Why promulgate it? Second, although the operation is simple, anaesthetizing a newly born kitten is an extremely skilled and delicate business. Third, removing the kitten from its mates and exposing it to strange odours all too often leads to its rejection when reintroduced to the litter. Fourth, the queen may resent any handling later and neglect the necessary post-operative care. Or if you insist on caring for the kitten as it should be cared for, the whole nursing procedure may be so upset that the mother may turn on a perfectly healthy kitten and mutilate or kill it. And fifth, as many litters contain too many kittens it is logical to cull those with obvious deformities. And sixth (I won't be popular for spelling this out yet again) there are too many kittens born everywhere. Why should we add to the problem those which Nature would eliminate?

I don't think it's a particularly instructive exercise to list all the possible deformities, abnormalities, and monstrosities that may be seen in the newborn of any species. When one considers the thousands of possible permutations as cells divide to become tissues and then further divide to become organs, the wonder is that the overwhelming percentage is so nearly perfect. All the more reason, then, to elimate those that would not survive without human help. Those who condemn this policy of rigid culling, saying that all life is precious and must be saved at all costs, take unto themselves the terrible responsibility of sustaining weaklings, throwbacks, freaks, and cripples that are fated to suffer lingering deaths the moment they are abandoned by man. Over the years I have met many sorts of people in animal welfare work. I couldn't begin to identify their various motives, but obviously the entire spectrum exists right from the sheer sentimentalist to the greedy, grasping and avaricious. I think I can fairly state that almost without exception after a few weeks of experience in a busy clinic the question is not whether some animals should be put to sleep, but how it can be done most painlessly.

There's no point in assisting a queen through the weeks of rearing kittens if you will be so desperate when they are weaned that you will allow them to go to unsuitable homes. Nor is there any point in rearing a kitten with, for example, a large umbilical hernia unless you are prepared, or you know someone who is prepared, to pay for the operation to have it rectified. A kitten may be born with one eye or many extra toes or a club foot or without claws. A kitten may be born with all or part of a limb missing, or it may have broken a leg during delivery and twisted it hopelessly. It simply doesn't make sense to rear creatures that may require extra attention all their lives if you are not prepared to grant such attention or to set up an adequate trust fund to keep the animal all its days. Do you find it ridiculous that trust funds should be set up for unwanted animals? Frankly, I do. But then I don't condemn people whose task it is to put unwanted and surplus animals to sleep.

Of course, it is one thing to decide to put a kitten to sleep and another to actually do it. Many people can't bring themselves to finish off a rat caught in a trap. Let me state first how I think it should *not* be done. *Drowning is both cruel and slow.* A kitten that bobs up after even three or four minutes of immersion and gasps another breath experiences anew the sensation of drowning.

Chloroform, properly administered, is a comfortable, painless way of doing the job. The proper way includes an adequate flow of air at the same time as the chloroform is placed in the box or bin with the kittens. If you place the kittens in a box with a chloroform-soaked rag they soon begin to suffocate – if you place them in a box with plenty of small air holes in it they just gradually nod off to sleep. You add more chloroform. The sleep gets deeper and deeper.

I prefer to inject a small amount of anaesthetic, such as sodium pentobarbitone. Admittedly the kitten does feel that initial prick, but afterwards it feels nothing as the sleep gets deeper and deeper.

What should be your procedure? If there's a veterinarian available and you can afford his fee, place the kittens in a small box and take them to him. If you can't afford the fee or the veterinarian is away, call your local R.S.P.C.A. or other animal welfare organization. Almost always there will be someone available who has the experience, the expertise, and the equipment to do the job.

A final word on that subject. Recently an international authority on the problem of stray cats and dogs suggested that wherever possible females should be culled and males saved. The reasons are obvious.

How can you tell a male from a female? It's not easy if you're any distance away. Males are, as a rule, slightly larger, but there are so many exceptions to this rule that for all practical purposes you can forget about it. The males also usually have larger, thicker heads and heavier well-muscled shoulders.

Cats that look like a blanket of red, black and yellow patches are called tortoiseshell – add white and they're calico. Almost always they are female. Ginger or marmalade cats (those with reddish stripes) are usually males; but you mustn't be surprised to find the occasional female ginger. A tortoiseshell male, on the other hand, is a genuine rarity, and more than likely will turn out to be sterile when it grows up.

Tabbys and blacks and whites and all the other colours can be either male or female, so that's not much help. If you handle the kitten gently and look under its tail you will see two small openings. The one at the top is the anus and it's the same in both males and females. The one below is the external organ of sex. In the female it's a tiny slit – in the male it's a tiny circle.

In young kittens it may be a bit difficult to tell the difference between the small 'i', which is what the female looks like, and the colon ':', which is what the male looks like. However, if you compare two or three members of a litter you'll soon get the idea.

Under the anus of the male kitten you can see a small sac. This small sac contains two round tiny pea-shaped testicles. It takes about eight months to a year before the testicles reach their full size. Then each of them may be as large as a grape. Male cats are called toms, females are called queens. I don't know why the males aren't called Dick or Harry but it must be rather nice, if female, to be called a queen.

Although these directions for telling the sex of a kitten appear simple and straightforward let me assure you that a sizeable proportion of otherwise sensible people simply cannot get the idea. Nor is it only newborn kittens that are mistakenly identified. At least once a month every veterinarian in small animal practice has a huge monster of a tomcat placed on his examination table with the earnest query, 'Is she pregnant, Doc?' or 'She's three years old! Why doesn't she have kittens?' Equally often, we are shown queens in the last few days of pregnancy and the owner says something like, 'Doctor, this is my tomcat Henry and there's sure something wrong with him. All he wants to do is eat and sleep and he's got so fat that he can hardly turn around to see which direction the mice are coming from.'

So don't cull on the basis of sex unless you are perfectly confident that you can tell one from the other. The same goes for colour. Many a litter of absolutely perfect Siamese kittens has been taken to the veterinarian with the request that they be put to sleep because they bore no markings. It is perfectly normal for Siamese to be born all white. The markings come later. If you are looking for tabbys or for calicoes or smokes or blues or any of the other intriguing possibilities, don't count your kittens and your disappointments until they're dry. As they emerge from their mother they look like nothing more than wet, bedraggled, formless, grey or mouse-coloured rodents. It is only after a few minutes of the mother's vigorous lick of life that they begin to gasp and take shape, and only after a proper clean-up and drying all over can one see markings and colours.

Remember too that eyes and ears are closed at birth and only open gradually after the first few days. The same is true of puppies. Too many have lost their lives because the owners thought that that protective device of Nature was an abnormality. Let me repeat. Culling is a serious business not to be undertaken lightly by the inexperienced breeder. If you are in doubt, better get in touch with an experienced breeder or preferably your veterinarian.

Many other problems may arise during those first few hours, of course, demanding decisions. Many of them can only be sorted out with the help of your veterinarian or your local animal welfare society. For example, many people know perfectly well that they will not be able to find homes for more than two kittens. The surplus should be put down without any qualms of conscience. I do think, however, that it's unfair to leave a mother cat with a single kitten. She will probably produce surplus milk and may develop a mastitis. Nor should a young kitten be deprived of the opportunity of learning to play with a brother or sister.

Sometimes there are ten or a dozen kittens and the owner is determined to rear them all. He or she is best advised to consult with the veterinarian from day one. Some prefer to leave the whole large litter on the mother for the first fortnight or three weeks, then wean half on to formula. Others claim – and often they are the ones with most experience – that it is better to start half of them on formula and artificial rearing at once.

There is one other consideration at this time. Many observers believe that a mother cat is perfectly capable of going out and getting pregnant again within seventy-two hours of bearing a litter. I have not found any scientific verification of this belief – but I have seen many litters born nine weeks and a day or two after a previous litter. It may be that the inhibition of mating and pregnancy which accompanies the flow of milk doesn't really get going for two or three days. I don't know. I do know, however, that many veterinarians (myself included) advise their clients to keep the mother cat indoors for at least three days after the birth of a litter.

I think that covers most of the exigencies and tragedies of the first two or three days. After that and until the third week when the gradual process called weaning begins there are relatively few problems. Provided the mother is fed an adequate (and adequately varied) diet, everything goes smoothly.

As the kittens grow larger they deplete the mother's resources even further. Even an average-sized litter may easily equal the weight of their mother, so you can realize just how much milk, and of what quality, she is producing. So throughout the nursing period, give her the same high quality foods that she received through pregnancy, with the emphasis on such high protein items as meat, fish, poultry, milk, eggs, and cheese. She must also receive adequate vitamin and mineral supplements. If, as in the case of so many Orientals, the nursing mother simply cannot be persuaded to take adequate quantities of milk you must make sure that she is getting enough minerals from the other items in her diet. Indeed, in some cases, it is necessary either to push vitamin and mineral pills down their unwilling throats or give them injections. Owners of such cats had better realize early that they cannot depend on any fad or herb to make good the deficiency. They had better work out a regime with their veterinarian and stick with it!

One of the illnesses which may strike during this early rearing period is flu. It looks not unlike a severe cold in the human. The eyes are red and full of discharge. The nose too may be discharging or it may be sore and crusted. The cat and her kittens may sneeze or cough and they may breathe in short rasping gasps. Any of those symptoms must almost always be taken very seriously. If neglected, a flu in a cat will develop into a bronchitis or a pneumonia. The mother cat may shake it off when she gets rid of her kittens or when the warm weather comes, but the young kittens will either die or be left with a chronic predisposition to respiratory trouble.

What is the cause? Usually it's a virus, but almost always the virus weakens the animal so much that many bacteria move in as well. Recent research shows that the virus may be any one of several dozen that cause flu in the human, or it may be one of several peculiar to the cat.

Early treatment, including antibiotic injections for the mother and usually for the kittens as well, is generally successful. Good nursing is very important too. That includes washing away all the discharges, using a teaspoonful of salt to a pint of water, and then dabbing the prescribed antibiotic in the eyes and around the sore and chapped nasal passages. If the mother is off her food because her sense of smell has been affected she may be encouraged to eat by offering her very strong cheese or fish with a strong odour. The kittens may have to be encouraged to nurse by holding them to the teats.

Sometimes within a day of the injections the cat and her kittens appear to make a miraculous recovery, and there's a strong temptation not to return to the veterinarian. If you succumb, whether through motives of economy or considerations of time, the animals will almost certainly relapse a day or two later, and with a vengeance. The treatment should be continued for at least forty-eight hours after the cessation of all symptoms. In fact, one researcher told me recently that he believes an adult cat that has suffered a case of flu with complications should be kept on antibiotics by mouth for at least thirty days.

Another condition that may strike during this initial period is, unhappily, usually not amenable to treatment even if recognized in its initial stages. This condition, which is called the 'fading kitten' or 'fading litter' syndrome, has its counterpart in other domesticated species and in some wild ones raised under zoo conditions. I have not see any references to the condition in wild animals in their natural environment, but it is a very widespread and worrying problem seen in young calves, pigs, lambs, and even more commonly in pure-bred puppies. I can think of no word better than 'fading' to describe those afflicted. It usually occurs within the first two or three days after birth, but it may occur later. The cry of the kitten changes from its normal strong, vociferous, and demanding tone to a weak, whining wail that deteriorates into a helpless squeak before death. Purposeful directed muscular contractions and movement of the limbs become flabby, undirected, and abortive. Almost before one's eyes the creature fades away. Its respiration becomes shallow and laboured. Its temperature drops and death releases it.

In practically all cases I have seen, the whole litter, whether of piglets, puppies or kittens, is affected. And despite all efforts the majority die.

What is the cause? It's still in dispute. Some scientists maintain that a specific virus is involved. Others say that it's a pathogenic form of a common bacteria commonly found in the gut called E. coli. Some say that although they don't know the exact cause they have proved that the injection of certain sera made from the blood of hyper-immune animals will prevent the condition from occurring. Others claim good results with injections given at the first sign of the condition. Let me say that, unlike flu or enteritis or many of the other conditions which we commonly see in the cat, there does not at this moment appear to be a common denominator found in all fading litters in all places. This is a condition which, at the moment, can only be treated by your local veterinarian according to local experience. In most places, results still leave much to be desired. In the London practices I know, despite wholehearted effort at the clinical level and early collaboration with laboratory veterinarians, the mortality rate still remains about 80 per cent. And three practices I visited recently in Canada reported similar unsatisfactory non-results.

This is obviously a fecund field for research. Aside from that going on in the commercial laboratories and in the universities, the Feline Advisory Bureau, a non-profit cat lovers' organization in England, finances a project to try to solve that problem among others.

I have underlined the woes only to contrast the joys. Given a good diet, a quiet corner in a warm house, and a modicum of common sense in their owners, the overwhelming majority of all queens rear their young without fuss. The queen emerges to eat and to attend to her own personal toilet, and if she's so inclined, to proudly display her kittens. Usually she carries them about by the scruff of their necks. Interestingly enough, this is not instinctive – it has to be perfected by experience. For the first few days a mother may carry her first litter around any which way. She may grab a kitten by its loin, its leg, or its abdomen. After a bit of trial and error she learns that the scruff is easier on the kitten and easier on her, putting a minimum of strain on both, and giving the mother a maximum of control.

The suckling kitten doesn't emerge from the nest until it's two or three weeks of age. Precocious kittens born to people-oriented mothers might emerge a day or two earlier than that while semi-wild kittens will stay hidden even longer. Till that time, its development is limited by the boundaries of its nest, and its activities are confined to interactions with its siblings and its mother.

Most of its time is spent suckling or sleeping. During that period, or at least the first twenty days of it, it is the mother who nuzzles the kittens from sleep to suckling wakefulness, and it is she who cradles them into warmth. When she leaves the nest, as leave it she must, they arrange themselves into a pattern depending on the temperature of the nest. If it is warm they spread themselves out; if it is cool they huddle in a symmetrical pattern so the head of one warms the flank of another.

When they are neither nursing nor sleeping (which is relatively seldom in the younger kitten but occurs more frequently and for longer periods as the kittens approach three weeks of age) they gradually learn to use their organs of locomotion, scent, sight, and hearing. By the time they are ready to emerge from the box they can recognize their mother and their brothers and sisters very well by odour and fairly well by sight. They have learned to snarl and hiss and to recognize a stranger. It is the sense of smell that must be most important in this recognition of danger for many kittens are hissing in a satisfactorily nasty manner at four days of age – well before their eyes are even partially opened. If you don't believe me pay them a visit without a prior introduction. Fair warning! If you don't know the mother, make sure she's not about when you try the experiment.

And although they're not particularly articulate they can be noisily rude. They have learned to recognize a few sounds like 'keep quiet, danger approaches' and 'Get away before I clout you, that's my nipple' and 'Stop that at once or you'll be sorry' and 'Ouch!' There may be others but I'll let you find them out for yourself.

Within the nest kittens learn to control their limbs. They learn to reach and grab and withdraw. Unsteadily they learn to crawl and walk and pounce. They're confined to a tiny nest but they learn all its possible lessons to perfection. They have to, because that confined classroom is the threshold of the great world outside.

2 The Orphan Kitten

Sometimes a queen takes her last breath as the kitten struggles with its first. Sometimes the mother becomes infected or torn and dies more slowly.

Occasionally when she leaves the nest she meets an unexpected and overwhelming force which prevents her return. Predators have been known to raid a nest and leave before all the occupants were dead.

Some queens produce no milk. Others have been known to kill all of their litter save one and the one has only survived through the blindness of uncontrollable emotion. Man may benignly decree that a queen can only comfortably care for a fraction of her offspring.

So far as I know no one has studied whether feral cats ever decide to rear some three or four offspring and reject the remainder. I have seen queens inexplicably push an apparently healthy kitten out of the nursing area and into the area of chilling death beyond. No matter how one attempts to foil and fool her often one cannot reverse her rejection.

Those are but some of the possible reasons why we may have an orphan on our hands. They exert considerable emotional influence even over the least sentimental of people. Few women find themselves able to refuse the appeal of an orphaned animal. I suspect that that appeal is universal and transcends the normal inhibitions between species. A helpless begging creature with wide-open jaws may be cared for by the most unlikely guardians. One scientist noted that goldfish that had learned to feed by the side of an outdoor pool were being fed by a group of cardinals that just couldn't pass those gaping mouths.

A nursing mother often needs little persuasion or none to accept a needy youngster. Some of these interspecific relationships don't stretch the foster mother's capacity over much; nor do they impose drastic changes on the orphan. Cats, rabbits, dogs, rats, mice, lions and tigers, wolves and foxes have all at one time or another figured in each other's permutations. Legends and myths abound of more unusual combinations. Over the centuries shepherds, herdsmen, and breeders have learned that the nursing female cares not at all about the looks of her prospective sucklers. If they smell familiar, she'll usually accept them. If they don't she may reject them or even attack the helpless creatures.

Common sense decrees that the best foster mother for an orphan kitten is a nursing queen. If she is at about the same stage of lactation as the natural mother would have been, so much the better. Failing a nursing queen, a nursing bitch of small or medium size may with a minimum of applied psychology be persuaded to accept a few kittens.

Simple methods will endow the orphans with an acceptable odour. Some say they should be rubbed with milk obtained from the foster mother. Others say her faeces or urine should be used. Some successful breeders who have had more than enough of the problem say that all that is necessary is to place the kittens in the nest while the foster mother is absent. In the horse and sheep world it is common practice to skin the hide off a dead colt or lamb and tie it around the orphan before presenting it to the nursing mother. Some people have successfully used the same method in cats.

However one confers an air of familiarity on the orphans, the takeover is often facilitated if the foster mother is not allowed to nurse for some hours beforehand. As the pressure of milk in her mammary glands builds up to the point of discomfort, she becomes less discriminating about who will have the privilege of relieving that discomfort. (I once sleepily overheard a discussion about that problem in the human – I say sleepily because it was part of a prolonged talk between the mother of my then newborn son and a friend who had gone through the procedure previously. I find most of these feminine exchanges of confidences repetitive and soporific. Nevertheless, I distinctly heard the following sentence: 'But, my dear, I simply couldn't wake her up so I grabbed some other brat who was screaming its head off and nursed it. I was in so much agony that I couldn't have cared less if the matron herself had come in at that moment and caught me.')

Once the foster mother allows the orphans to nurse she seldom rejects them later; in fact, usually that single mutual action often appears to bond them as firmly as blood.

Where a foster mother is not available, however, the kittens must be raised artificially. If you are prepared to spend a little money and effort in providing the proper equipment, there is no reason why you shouldn't succeed in rearing a high percentage of the orphans. Make no mistake about one thing, however. The queen spends several hours a day at the job and no fancy formulae or new-fangled inventions can turn those necessary hours into minutes. Sometimes a burst of teenage enthusiasm convinces a family to embark on the life-saving venture. Too often a tired mother decides that she can't cope another day and takes the orphans off to the veterinarian. Needless to say it's a harder and harsher decision after a week or two of effort, satisfaction, and pride.

The most common cause of death among orphan kittens in the first day or two is chilling. You *must* provide the proper environment. There's no point in guessing. Rig up a proper thermometer. Place it near the kittens and at their level. For the first twenty-four hours the temperature should be 90° Fahrenheit. For the next four or five days the ideal temperature is 85° Fahrenheit, and after that the temperature can be dropped to 80° until the kittens are two weeks old. From then on they may be maintained at 70°.

As in everything to do with animals, various experts favour various systems. One devised for puppies at the New York State Veterinary College at Cornell University has been extensively tried and proven by many cat breeders to rear orphan kittens. They suggest a temperature of from 85° to 90° for the first five days, gradually decreasing to 80° by the seventh to the tenth day, and further gradual reductions to 75° by the end of the fourth week.

You needn't call out the Fire Department if the temperature rises above 92° – nor do you start a bonfire if it momentarily drops to 65°. In other words, these recommended temperatures are simply meant to give you an idea of the goal. They are not absolute requirements. If you follow them as a general guide and use your common sense, it is unlikely that a kitten will be overheated to exhaustion or chilled beyond the point of no return. And keep in mind that, like ourselves, even the most delicate of kittens can endure fair bit of discomfort without sustaining any harm. It has been suggested, in fact, that a bit of rigour in early life may lead to greater vigour later on.

Obviously the best way to provide a suitable environment is to buy or build or rig up a proper incubator. One of the best sorts is a modification of the old-fashioned chicken incubator. These are about the height and size of an ordinary card table. (Obviously it's much, much easier if you don't have to stoop.) The actual incubator is about six inches deep. Underneath are a couple of electric heating elements and a thermostat. Inside is an easily read thermometer. The top is a hinged door of glass. Along the sides there are holes adequate for ventilation. The whole setup need cost no more than the cost of a single purebred kitten.

Beware, however, of the more old-fashioned paraffin- or oil-heated incubator. Aside from the risk of fire, these unless tended constantly may give off fumes which will asphyxiate the kittens, and if they operate with a wick are almost impossible to regulate. If there is no electricity (and some very nice parts of the civilized world are without it), you may convert to one form or other of bottled gas. Provided it is properly vented, it is safer and easier to control than oil or paraffin.

Some veterinarians suggest that an ordinary heating pad under a towel adjusted to give a medium heat is all that's required. Cover the heating pad with a good layer or layers of towelling.

Another simple incubator can be rigged by suspending a forty-watt bulb in a wooden box. The bulb should be kept at least six inches away from the kittens, and as they get older the temperature can be lowered by raising the bulb.

Some people prefer to go to the slight additional expense of an infra-red lamp, which has the advantage of not disturbing the kittens once their eyes are open. It is suspended a foot or two feet above the kittens, according to the recorded temperature.

Until you can rig up something more elaborate, a hot water bottle will prevent the kittens from becoming chilled and dying. If it's 3.00 in the morning and you discover that the stopper must have been buried with Grannie, then you may substitute a plastic bottle filled with hot water. Wrap it in a towel.

Finally the simplest system of all is to raise the temperature of the whole room. I once visited a home in which a litter of orphan kittens were being successfully reared. The whole house was unbearably hot. 'It keeps the kittens happy and my husband unhappy,' said the proud lady. 'The only disadvantage is that I can't stand heat.'

You might hire a platoon of engineers to regulate the temperature and still lose the kittens simply because they are not getting the proper amount of rest. The only way to ensure this vital ingredient of survival is to separate the kittens. It is often difficult to convince people of the necessity for this. They feel that the kittens, having lost their mother, need each other's company more than ever. They point out that a litter of kittens that are feeling chilly will automatically cuddle up to each other, and if they're feeling too hot will automatically spread themselves out. That slight advantage, however, doesn't outweigh the fact that they will disturb each other. As a kitten wakes it begins to suckle its neighbour. The neighbour wakes and turns on a third. They no sooner finish and drop off to sleep when a fourth wakes and the cycle is repeated.

Those small rectangular plastic dishes commonly used to store vegetables in the bottom of refrigerators make ideal containers for individual kittens. They come in a variety of sizes. Those about six or eight inches wide and three or four, or better yet five, inches high are ideal. They are cheap and easily cleaned. They are easily obtainable. Small shops in remote jungles and igloo trading posts keep a large selection in all sizes and most colours.

Another aid is an alarm clock placed near the sleeping kittens. One theory is that it will remind them of their mother's heartbeat, and thus bring comfort and a sense of well-being into their lives. Another is that any quiet regular sound near by tends to reassure by rendering distant occasional noises less important and thus less alarming. Needless to say, you won't enhance the soothing quality of the tick-tock if you forget to shut off the alarm.

The best bedding material is shredded cellulose or a couple or three layers of fairly thick paper tissues. On those materials it's easy to inspect the droppings. Should you need to measure the excreta it is easy to weigh the tissues before and after. Neither shavings nor sawdust make suitable bedding as the aspiration of wood dust may cause pneumonia. Whatever bedding is used should be changed at least daily.

Another important piece of equipment is a set of scales. An egg-grading scale is an excellent method of weighing very small kittens.

Feline milk is perhaps the highest in terms of protein content of all the milks produced by our domestic animals. For this reason it is difficult to use milk substitutes that are made for humans or dogs as a milk replacer for kittens. One formula which has proven successful is as follows:

Two tablespoons condensed milk
Two tablespoons boiled water
¼ teaspoon corn syrup
¼ teaspoon Bovril or other bouillon concentrate

Many people find it much more simple and get equally good results by using tinned unsweetened evaporated milk just as it comes from the tin. This is not condensed milk. I repeat. It is unsweetened evaporated (and preferably irradiated) tinned milk. Best of all are the powdered formulae especially manufactured for kittens.

Incidentally, many authorities cannot agree on the correct frequency of feeding. Many claim that it's absolutely essential to feed every hour. One researcher in a German laboratory achieved very good results with only three daily feedings. Others agree with the three- or four-hourly interval as outlined above, but stretch the night-time break to eight hours after the first week.

There are some complicated formulae used for figuring out exactly how much one should be feeding per day at different stages of a kitten's development. All of them are based on the general rule that the average kitten should receive about 250 calories for every 2.2 pounds that it weighs. That is when it is four weeks of age; during the first week its requirements are only about 195 calories per kilogramme. In practice if you ignore those complicated calculations and start with about one and a half teaspoonfuls at each four-hourly feeding and gradually increase the amount you won't go far wrong. Some kittens will take all they need or want in five minutes. Most take about ten. If they are crying after you think they've had enough either it's been spilled and wasted or the formula is not rich enough. If you weigh the kitten at the same time every day and the chart shows a steady increase then you can't be going very far wrong.

A more convenient but more expensive way of feeding the kittens is to purchase one of the ready-made products specifically formulated to replace the milk of the mother cat. Better pet shops usually have a fair selection, or your veterinarian can usually name a local source. Take the added trouble – even if it is a terrible bore – to get one that categorically states that it is for cats. The orphan kitten faces sufficient struggle for survival without being faced with the additional handicap of trying to survive on an unsuitable diet.

It might survive on a milk formulated for a human baby, but that doesn't eliminate the fact that until it is weaned on to solids it will have suffered from a kind of semi-starvation.

The newborn kitten should gain about 10 grammes the first day. Experience has proved that to do so it must ingest at least an ounce of the milk mixture – roughly two and a half tablespoons – in the first twenty-four hours. This means a minimum of one teaspoonful every three hours. As the kitten takes more than one teaspoonful at a feed you can gradually cut those feedings down. Many people find that by the end of the second or third day the kittens are taking one and a half teaspoonfuls at a feed, and so only need to be fed every four hours.

It is sometimes very difficult to teach the kittens how to suckle an artificial feeder. It is always easier to raise them artificially from the first day than it is to change them to the bottle after a few days of natural nursing. There are several sorts of bottles that one may try. Among the most satisfactory are those with an olive-shaped expansion of the teat and a constriction between the teat and the base. They are now being stocked by good pet shops. If these are unobtainable you can use a doll's bottle with a nipple that actually works. Some people would prefer to stick to the old-fashioned eye dropper with a glass bulb on the tip which gives the kitten something to suck on. You must not, of course, use the rubber bulb portion to force milk into the kitten. Let the kitten suck it out. In other words the bulb on the eye dropper is used to fill the tube but not the kitten. The danger is that too much milk will be forced into the kitten and choke it. Sadly, many many artificially raised kittens develop a pneumonia from this cause and die before they are four or five days old.

At each feed the formula should be warmed to a temperature of about 100° Fahrenheit. The 'operator' or 'nurse' should be comfortably seated during the procedure. There is no point in half kneeling or half bending over the incubator and trying to bend the kitten's neck to the right angle with one hand and direct the bottle with the other. The kitten should be placed on one's lap! Naturally, that lap is protected by a thick towel. That rough towel affords a measure of protection to its possessor and confers no small security to the tiny kitten, which must claw a precarious purchase on that towel while being partially supported by the palm of the human 'parent'. While the kitten rests on the human palm its head is directed in the right direction by an index finger and thumb. Sometimes the proffering hand with its attendant bottle and nipple have little appeal. In that case, a drop of the formula on the nose of the hungry orphan may initiate the reflex lick that will give it the idea. More often the suckling reaction is initiated by inserting and withdrawing the bottle with one hand while gently pressing the nipple ever so slightly with the other. Be careful! A large drop may be too much. The idea is to simply moisten the mouth and give the kitten the idea. If your slight squeeze is followed by a bout of gasping or coughing put the bottle aside and elevate the kitten's hindquarters so that it can easily expel the bit that went down the wrong way.

I know all this must sound terribly precise and, as in Victorian novels, fraught with danger. Let me reassure you that after a single session with each of six kittens even the most nervous and inexperienced orphan nursery attendants will be able to give these instructions better than I.

After the kitten has finished its ration hold it on its back in the palm of your hand and give its tummy a rub with your finger in order to help expel any air that may have been ingested. Then you must simulate the absent mother by gently massaging the whole area under its tail with a piece of clean cloth or a tissue dipped in lukewarm water. This stimulates the evacuation reflex and the kitten will usually urinate. After half a dozen kittens have successfully completed this automatic response, you will understand why I specified a towel as a protective covering. Afterwards the area should be patted dry with some soft tissue and a thin layer of Vaseline or petrolatum or proprietary nappy ointment spread over the area.

Solid motions, however, may or may not be passed at the time of that gentle massage. Usually they are passed at intervals throughout the day and night. The pattern seems to be variable, but you can be sure that if you have just cleaned out its plastic home and relined it with paper the kitten will pick that moment.

In colour the motions resemble nothing so much as the formula being fed, but don't be alarmed by variations in hue. At the beginning (as the formula is mainly milk) you can expect the faeces to be creamy or grey in colour. Later, as meat and other animal proteins are added, you can logically expect the faeces to darken.

The consistency of the motion in an average healthy kitten should be neither too runny nor too firm. I don't mean to upset those people who spend thousands of pounds advertising their wonderful products, but the consistency of the faeces of a normal kitten is most easily described as resembling toothpaste as it is squeezed from the tube.

If the kitten is constipated, insert the large end of a greased toothpick about a quarter of an inch into the rectum. If the bowels are too loose cut down the amount of syrup or other liquids in the formula. If either condition persists for more than twenty-four hours or the kitten appears to be in pain, have a word on the telephone with your veterinarian.

The eyes should be cleaned at least once daily. They may be gently swabbed with a bit of cotton soaked in normal saline (teaspoon of salt to a pint of water) or with boracic acid solution which your chemist can easily formulate or with a good grade of medicinal mineral oil. Naturally, eyes that appear unduly sticky must be examined by the veterinarian.

The kittens should be taught to lap as soon as possible. Again some experts suggest that three and a half weeks is the earliest time for the switchover, but many a kitten has started lapping at two weeks of age without any ill effects. All changeovers must be made gradually. You shouldn't, for example, try to introduce the kittens to lapping and meat on the same day. Place the usual formula on a saucer or petri dish. Make sure it's warmed to the usual temperature. Offer it to the kitten at a normal feeding time. Dip the kitten's nose in the mixture. Keep one hand behind the kitten, as its first reaction will be to back away. If you allow it to back up it will then have difficulty in associating the saucer with the source of food. Some kittens get the idea very quickly. Within a half a minute or so they're licking the stuff off their nose and lips and looking for more. Others take a bit longer. If a kitten looks as if it's not going to get the idea that day postpone the whole procedure for three or four days and try again.

It is very important to wash and boil those saucers and petri dishes as meticulously as you do the feeding bottles and nipples. Milk is an ideal medium for bacterial growth and any sloppiness in the handling of milk and utensils will lead to gastric infection.

After a kitten has been lapping for three or four days you can add finely chopped minced beef or finely chopped and minced cooked fish to the mixture. (Some owners feed their young kittens on Farex or other cereals, but they have a tendency to create potbellies because the kittens must eat too much to get their protein requirements.) Gradually increase the amount of meat and decrease the amount of fluid. At the end of five weeks the kittens should be having either two or three solid meals a day.

The kitten must receive at least 1,000 international units of vitamin A per day. Check the label on the condensed milk to see how much vitamin A it contains, then supplement it with the appropriate amount of cod liver oil.

I hope that the preceding pages of detailed instructions will have abundantly illustrated the fact that the rearing of orphaned young is neither play nor a temporary diversion for idle children. It is far more difficult to artificially feed a tiny kitten than it is to give a baby a bottle. How can you rationalize the folly of allowing a young child whom you wouldn't allow to feed a baby to try and nurse an animal? I'm not trying to equate the life of an animal with that of a human, but it elevates neither if the life of one is sacrificed to satisfy a momentary urge of the other. Let me put it more bluntly. Inept hands can drown a kitten. In an unthinking moment a window may be left open and a litter chilled to death. Too commonly a squirming kitten is dropped from an uncertain grip, fracturing a leg if it's lucky, its spine if it's not. These accidents can happen with experienced and careful adults. How much more likely are they to happen if children are left in charge?

I'm not at all suggesting that children should be excluded from the very real satisfactions and joys of the venture. They should, of course, be encouraged to participate within the limits of their ability and responsibility. But every step of the procedure should be supervised, and a child should be left in charge of even a minor task only when he has amply demonstrated that he knows exactly what to do. These precautions are not solely for the benefit of the kittens. Many a child has suffered considerable anguish at the realization that his own inadvertence has maimed or killed a living creature.

Some experienced people say that the best age to reunite the litter is just after the eyes are open, at say ten, twelve, or fourteen days of age. Others say that it is best to keep them separated until five or six weeks of age. The ideal compromise would seem to be to introduce them to each other when they are lapping without difficulty. At three weeks of age they generally will adjust to each other's strange presences without difficulty. At that stage too they may be introduced to a maternally inclined non-nursing cat. That pleasant creature, if it's so inclined, will teach the litter many of the important lessons of life.

With our modern formulae and equipment the task of physically raising the orphan is much easier than it used to be. I see few with apparent physical defects as a result of the deprivations of artificial rearing. I do see, however, too many that never get over the lack of contact with others of their kind until too late.

One study of kittens that were reared separately in incubators showed that they were not too unlike their more fortunate cousins that were reared naturally. They seemed, however, to be slightly more active and considerably more noisy. One investigator suggests that this means that they are searching for nutrition and warmth.

Another study showed that such incubator-raised kittens

and kittens that were taken from their mother at two weeks of age were more likely to show anxiety in new situations than normal kittens. And although they were more aggressive, they were less successful in competition for food. They were also slower in learning a simple feeding routine.

We know from many studies of naturally reared kittens that for the first three weeks they tend to stay in one corner of their box and spend most of their time either nursing or sleeping. It is after the third week that the kittens start to play with each other and wander away. This further reinforces my recommendation to reunite the litter at three weeks of age. Breeders that have listened to this advice report that such orphans manage to grow up without any apparent neuroses and anxieties.

Orphan kittens that are raised as individuals and are not introduced to their own kind until they are half grown may not necessarily be backward, but they will almost certainly be extremely nervous of other animals and extremely dependent on their human master. It is the height of cruelty to ever allow such a kitten to get in a situation where it must fend for itself.

You must remember that orphan kittens, having no opportunity to pick up immunity through the medium of the mother's early milk (colostrum), are therefore much more susceptible to infection. Your veterinarian may suggest that in these circumstances it is safer to inaugurate a course of inoculations beginning at four or five weeks of age.

May I end on a happy note? There is no aspect of animal husbandry that requires more constant watchfulness and attention to detail than the handrearing of orphans. By the end of the third or fourth day some people who have embarked on such a venture look in the mirror and wonder if what they see is the face of a fool. After a further week they stop wondering because they're sure that it is. But by the end of the third week, as one grows increasingly fond of the developing and individual personalities, one smiles smugly. There are many ways of making a fool of oneself, but few are rewarded with quite so much satisfaction.

3 The Kitten in Trouble

Watch a kitten enter a room for the first time. Watch, as its apprehension is overcome by its curiosity. This in turn is tempered by a caution which becomes confidence only after a thorough survey has revealed that the area is safe.

But how safe is it? Kittens appear to instinctively recoil from some dangers like the edge of a great precipice or the banks of a fast-flowing stream or the menacing growls of a dog. But they have no way of knowing that the large metal object from which emanates the delightful aroma of food is covered with four circles of fire. Nor do they know that the delightful black rubber cord coming from the wall contains within it another sort of fire.

I include this chapter (a catalogue of woes) not to depress but to instruct. A little thought and a little knowledge can do much to prevent accidents and alleviate pain.

As most kittens are fed in the kitchen the stove and its burden of cooking pots are an ever present source of danger.

This is one room in the house in which kittens must not be allowed above floor level. You can't expect a kitten to know that it is ever so sweet and clever to roll an orange across the table but nothing but filthy to walk across the lobster mayonnaise. Nor is it fair to allow it to explore a cold stove unless you are quite certain that every time a burner is on you will be in the vicinity to shoo the kitten away. Kittens are amenable to training. From the first day in its new home it must be firmly told – and shown if necessary – that it's perfectly welcome in the kitchen so long as it keeps its paws firmly on the floor.

How is it done? It depends on the kitten. My cat Moss hates any loud sudden sound. It took only about a week of vigilance and clapping at the opportune moment to teach him for ever that food-laden tables, refrigerators, and stoves were none of his affair. Belinda, the gentlest Siamese of all time, is not frightened of anything in the noise department. I'm sure that if the Mafia were to raid our drug cupboard with all guns blazing she would watch the proceedings with an expression of amused detachment. She cannot, however, stand any form of physical rebuke however gentle. The first time I caught her on the kitchen table daintily scooping up my scrambled eggs I picked her up by the scruff, slapped her twice (very softly) across the flank, and pushed her outdoors. She didn't come back for twelve hours and never again did she violate the rules of the kitchen.

But, let me confess (and I wish more 'experts' would do the same) that I have had my failures. Given half a chance my fat cat Malcolm would open the oven door and remove an entire turkey. On countless occasions he has managed to tip a hot frying pan over the edge of the stove. And he usually manages to pick up the most succulent bits while I am throwing my orange juice in the direction of his disappearing tail. I've tried everything but firecrackers and real live guns to dissuade him, and I have concluded that he's just a plain hungry cat. He was born that way. And I'm sure that when he dreams, he dreams of a cat heaven which is a giant supermarket absolutely full to bursting with all sorts of goodies being served up by an efficient and ingratiating staff to Himself who is the one and only customer.

On one occasion Malcolm leapt towards a paintbrush in my hand. He may have thought it was a new kind of sausage. He was so surprised by the taste of the paint that he leapt backwards, knocking a tin of turpentine over one of his hind legs and his tail. I immediately instituted vigorous first-aid treatment. I half filled the sink with lukewarm water, added soapflakes (green soap is better but I didn't have any handy), and tried to get as much off as quickly as I could. At the same time I took a paper towel and tried to wipe most of the paint off his tongue and lips. I don't know if he suffered more from the pain of the first-degree burns or from the injuries to his dignity.

Although the mouth was sore and painful he managed a fair meal of mashed meat the following day, blended in an electric mixer to the consistency of a thick soup. Any of the liquid or gelatine meat, veal, or chicken extracts would have done as well. I also applied an ointment which contains several different antibiotics and vitamins. This ointment (manufactured by a Canadian company and widely available in both Britain and America) is really designed for the treatment of enteritis in small animals. As it's meant to be taken internally I find it extremely useful for the treatment of many skin injuries and ailments in cats, whose every instinct is to lick everything extraneous off their coats. If one were to use the ordinary ointments designed for external use only, they just might cause more trouble than they were meant to cure.

As a first-degree burn is a mild one, just affecting the upper layers of the skin, quite often no other treatment than that I used on Malcolm for his paint and turpentine injuries is necessary. Sometimes four or five days after the event the affected area breaks out in painful blisters. Many veterinarians report that they get good results by treating such cases with penicillin and cortisone injections. They may also dispense pethidine or some other painkiller (but never aspirin, which is poisonous for cats).

If Malcolm had swallowed much turpentine or if it had been allowed to remain on the skin he would have suffered a severe colic. He would have been violently sick and later he would have had diarrhoea. He might have had nervous symptoms including dizziness, alternating with periods of frenzy and culminating in a coma. If he had swallowed a fair bit of the paint he might have shown similar symptoms as well as those associated with lead poisoning. I'll discuss various forms of first-aid for that sort of poisoning later on.

Second-degree burns are those that affect the deeper layers of the skin. Almost always they cause a fair bit of blistering and a great deal of discomfort and pain.

One of the common causes of such burns is spilling or leaking acid from a car battery. Get some baking soda, mix it liberally in a pail of water, and place or throw the cat into the pail. If the offending substance is caustic like washing soda, chloride of lime, or lye, use boracic acid instead of washing soda. If you have no idea what has caused the burn but the cat is obviously in agony quickly dilute the mess with as much water as you can apply. At that juncture there is no point in applying ointments. Wrap as much clean soft cloth around the patient as you have or as much as it will let you, place it in a basket, close the lid firmly, make sure it's escape-proof and then get on the telephone to a veterinarian.

Even a fairly small kitten can be a formidable handful when aroused. And nothing arouses any creature to the limits of its capacity as much as extreme pain combined with fear. If the kitten has been covered with some corrosive substance you must take every precaution to make sure that it doesn't transfer any to you or to any other innocent observers. I know a kind lady who lost the sight of an eye while rescuing a kitten from a pail of lye.

Nor do I have to stretch my memory to recall the Sunday morning that a neighbourhood antique dealer phoned. He kept a large vat of caustic soda lime in which wooden furniture was immersed to strip it of unwanted layers of paint. Someone had forgotten to put the protective cover over the vat and his cat had fallen in. It had managed to extricate itself almost immediately but that long second was long enough. There was no doubt that the cat would die. The question was how to effect that death as soon as possible. Even if the owner had had a gun, a screaming writhing cat covered in caustic is hardly a hazard-free indoor target for even the coolest of professional marksmen.

The method we used was not without its drawbacks. The cat was pinned to a corner with an ordinary broom. Then an apple box was clamped over the cat. As the apple box went down the broom was removed. Then a piece of plywood was inserted along the floor to create a completely enclosed box. This was tied securely and the whole was removed to my premises. There the nozzle of an anaesthetic machine was introduced into a knot hole. Doubtless there are other ways of dealing with such emergencies. That one took less than ten minutes from the time of the first anguished phone call until I could be sure that the cat was no longer feeling pain. One must, in those cases, try to quickly figure a method which is both efficient and safe.

That rather horrifying example helps put other sorts of emergencies into perspective. For example many people seeing their kitten with a slight limp panic and rush madly to the veterinarian. I recall one gentleman who came bursting in, almost apoplectic with anxiety. 'Roberta's broken her leg!' he shouted. It took some calm reassuring and further questioning to ascertain that Roberta was a fourteen-week-old white Persian and that in the urgency of the exigency he had left her at home.

Fractures – and suspected fractures – are a common feature of kittenhood. Considering the feats they attempt it would be surprising indeed if this were not so. One often sees a kitten climb up an eight-foot curtain, twist awkwardly, and drop with a thud that you'd swear must break every bone in its body. It gives itself a slight shake, walks away with a heroic limp, and twenty minutes later has apparently forgotten all about it. The law of averages, however, cannot be flouted indefinitely. If after an awkward fall the kitten refuses to put any weight on the foot or if the leg is dangling at an awkward angle you must catch it as gently and as quickly as possible and confine it in a small cage or secure basket. Get someone to help you before you attempt any further examination, and proceed only after you have cleared a room of children, dogs, and other cats. Have the assistant hold the kitten by the scruff of the neck with one hand while supporting its weight by cradling its chest in the other, and study the suspected limb. Does it look like its mate? Is it the same length? Does it hang the same way? If you suspect a front leg fracture move the kitten towards the edge of the table. It will instinctively grab the edge of the table, and if it pulls itself forward with the suspect limb you can be fairly sure that it's not fractured. If a hind leg has sustained the injury raise the kitten's chest so that all of its weight is carried on its own hind end. If it puts only one leg down and winces when the other approaches the table top you must suspect the worst. On the other hand if the kitten puts weight on a limb it's probably not broken.

That's as far as home treatment and home diagnosis should go. Do not attempt to feel or manipulate the limb. Do not attempt to splint or strap it. You will almost certainly do more harm than good. You have already instituted the best possible home aid; that is, you have reassured the kitten with a gentle touch, and most important of all you have confined it so it can't do itself any further injury.

Then, although it is prudent and kind to get the kitten to the veterinarian in a reasonable time, there is no reason whatsoever for either panic or emergency measures. Let me assure you that in many veterinary practices all that will be done for one or two or even three days will be the regular injection of painkillers (if they are needed), vitamin-mineral injections or supplements, and an X-ray or two if that seems indicated.

One busy metropolitan animal hospital I know finds that over 30 per cent of their kitten fractures respond well to the following regime: (a) confinement in a small cage for two to four weeks; (b) injections of painkillers if they are needed for the first few days; and (c) high level of vitamins and minerals in the diet and/or injections of the same.

Everyone who has lived with a cat has noticed how much heat they not only tolerate but actively enjoy. Have you ever tried to hold your hand to the radiator on which your cat is sleeping? I have, and quite often I can't. Despite their love of heat, however, cats can and do suffer from heat exhaustion if they are confined in a hot area without adequate ventilation. Kittens can find their way to the most improbable attic corners. Sometimes they get wedged under a stove or behind a furnace. And all over the world kittens may be exposed in shop windows to the rays of the sun.* The symptoms of heat exhaustion are rapid panting, drooling, and a worried anxious expression. The kitten stands with its head down, its mouth open, and its tongue protruding. Later it becomes weak and drops to the ground with its back arched and its legs stiff. At that stage its breathing will be very weak and the lips and gums will appear blue.

You probably won't remember all that, but remember the following. If you enter a room that is uncomfortably hot and you see a creature that is breathing very rapidly in shallow gasps you may save its life by plunging it into the coldest pail of water or ice and water available. Please try to remember too (amazing how many people don't) to remove the patient to a cooler area before you start looking for the ice and cold water. And, as cold water enemas and salt water injections are often used to treat the condition, the sooner you move to a veterinary establishment the better.

Although kittens (except the unhappy Rex) come equipped with efficient fur coats they can and do meet extremes of cold with which their tender bodies cannot cope. The initial freezing blast is uncomfortable but the actual process of freezing is distinguished by nothing so much as a lack of sensation. It's the thawing afterwards that is so painful. Remember that when trying to treat a victim of the cold. Whether just the tip of a tail or an ear is involved or an entire limb or

* In Holland, where a pet shop operator must take courses and pass examinations before receiving a licence, this doesn't happen—at least not in a pet shop!

the whole creature, the pain may be intense. The kitten should be placed in a warm room, not hot, a pethidine or other analgesic tablet administered, and a soothing antibiotic ointment sparingly rubbed into the affected tissues. And try to get it to a veterinary hospital as soon as possible.

Kittens love to play with string or cord. If a kitten bites into a live electric cord it may bite back – and with a vengeance. Be careful! The jolt of electricity may have caused the kitten to urinate. As you rescue it you may step in the pool and be electrocuted. Take that extra second to shut the current off at the switch. If the kitten has stopped breathing apply artificial respiration. Usually the inside of the mouth and tongue are badly burned at the same time, and your veterinarian will treat that area as outlined above for first- and second-degree burns.

Kittens may swallow lengths of material like butcher's cord, sewing thread, or string. A day or two later you will see the kitten straining to pass a short length of the material. Don't rush into a great tugging match. You may do more harm than good. Again look for an assistant, a table, and a good light. With the assistant holding the kitten, tug ever so gently on the cord. Sometimes it will come away without any effort at all. More often it seems to be tightly lodged. If you pull it too hard you may easily cause a prolapse. Leave it alone! If there's more than two inches emerging cut the surplus off with a pair of scissors. Otherwise the kitten may pull at it and do itself an injury. Then get on the phone to your veterinarian. He will probably hospitalize the kitten, give it one of those expanding cellulose products designed for cases of mild constipation, and hope that that will pass through easily carrying the cord with it. Or he may decide to X-ray and operate. Leave it to him! Even if he only graduated the day before yesterday you can be sure he knows more than you and this book put together. Why? Because he knows the principles of diagnosis and treatment and he's got your kitten (which is very much an individual) right there on the table in front of him.

Sometimes, even in the least domestic of homes, attached to

thread there is a needle. The kitten plays with the thread, swallows it, feels a twinge of sudden pain, and then tries to dislodge the sharp object which has become wedged in its throat. Unless you are very deft do not attempt to remove it without an assistant and a pair of fine pliers or forceps which clamp shut. With the assistant immobilizing the kitten fore and aft use one hand to pry open its mouth. Be gentle. If you can see where each end of the needle lies and you are quite sure there's no thread going down the gullet then clamp it with the forceps and remove. If it appears to be solidly wedged or if you are not quite sure what's happening to the other end, then leave it alone! Put the kitten in a basket and take it to the veterinarian. Over half of the needles which I have seen removed from the mouths of cats have been there at least twelve hours. A colleague told me of a case in which the needle lay diagonally at the back of the throat so that the kitten's mouth was kept about a quarter of an inch ajar. It could neither open it further nor close it tight. It had been 'under treatment' by the local pet shop for over a week. Without even seeing the kitten they had diagnosed it as arthritis due to a mineral deficiency and dispensed drops to be placed in the corner of the mouth! After the needle was removed the kitten made an uneventful recovery. As I said, there are emergencies and there are emergencies.

Now I must ask you to be indulgent while I try to simplify one of the most complicated branches of modern veterinary medicine. Toxicology – the branch of medicine which deals with poisons – now includes not only the classical drugs which the ladies in history books used to get rid of their unwanted lovers but the myriad of artificial food additives, antiseptics, disinfectants, and soaps we are constantly using, the pollutions we are constantly breathing, and the plethora of drugs which enrich the manufacturer and impoverish society.

No table, however lengthy and complicated, can do any more than give you an idea of how to suspect a case of poisoning and what to do about it until you can get to the veterinarian. The diagnosis of the specific poison and the choice of the most effective antidote these days requires a specialist with many years of training and the mind of a computer. I'm not exaggerating. In London today, one of the giant hospital complexes has a toxicology unit which provides a service for doctors and veterinarians. If a case of suspected poisoning isn't straightforward we call them, outline the possible sources and the symptoms, and ask them what to do next. The point is if we professionals need even more expert help all that an intelligent owner can do is (a) keep all potentially harmful substances out of Puss's reach; (b) if you suspect that she has swallowed poison gather up all the harmful substances that she could have come in contact with and take them along to the veterinarian with her; and (c) keep a supply of the 'universal antidote' in your medicine cabinet.

Let's start with the third because that's the simplest. Ask your chemist to mix you up a three- or four-ounce bottle. The formula most commonly used is two parts powdered charcoal (in an emergency you can use burnt toast instead), one part milk of magnesia and one part tannic acid or strong tea. This mixture cannot do any harm, and in many sorts of poisoning it can save a life. It is so efficient that it can absorb up to fifteen times its own weight of coal-tar poison and over a hundred times its own weight of strychnine. Try to get at least a tablespoonful or two down a kitten's throat and at least twice that much down an adult cat's.

What are the common dangerous poisons? May I repeat, the main value of the following list is as an indication of the substances that one must treat with respect. The rat and mouse poisons include strychnine, red and white squill, thallium, antu, warfarin, and sodium fluoroacetate, which is also known as 10.80. Each of those substances poisons rodents in its own particular fashion and each causes a different set of symptoms in the cat. As pet owners (who know full well that a cat can hardly be dissuaded from hunting, playing with, and occasionally eating rats or mice) we must make it our business to know which particular poison is being used in the locality. If you know what it is you can look up the symptoms and treatment and act accordingly.

STRYCHNINE

Mixed with canary seed and sold as mouse bait. Also still the favourite weapon of the malicious poisoner.

Early treatment is nearly always successful. It involves anaesthetizing the cat until the effects of the drug wear off.

RED AND WHITE SQUILL

Symptoms include vomiting, weakness, dizziness, and paralysis.

There is no specific treatment. Symptomatic treatment (treatment of each symptom as it occurs) is usually successful.

THALLIUM

Usually used by professional rat exterminators.

Symptoms include sores and incrustations around the lips and head, severe diarrhoea, muscular weakness and dizziness and a stilted unco-ordinated walk.

There is a specific antidote called Dithizone (Diphenylthiocarbazone).

ANTU

The most deadly of all rodent poisons. Death occurs very rapidly.

Symptoms include vomiting and difficult breathing followed by intense coughing which is caused by the fluids released into the chest cavity. Be careful! The bowels and chest are extremely painful and an affected animal resents handling.

Treatment is generally unavailing.

WARFARIN

The most commonly used of all rat and mouse poisons. It prevents the blood from clotting and the animal dies from numerous small haemorrhages. Warfarin poisoning is said to be painless. I don't know what the manufacturer's definition is of pain but I was once poisoned with the stuff and I'd sooner walk over hot coals. The first doctor I saw diagnosed it as lumbago. The second did numerous tests and said it was kidney stones. That was in Spain. I flew to a hospital in England where the first doctor was nonplussed but his chief came up with the answer after a few hours.

Treatment is usually successful (thank goodness) and includes injections of Vitamin K.

SODIUM FLUOROACETATE (10.80)
A highly potent poison that affects all animals. It is easily dissolved and is odourless and tasteless.

Symptoms are sudden in onset. The animal will cry in pain and then go into seizures. These seizures are particularly violent, right from the start.

There is no known treatment.

A second large group of poisons is that which includes the herbicides (substances with which man is trying to eliminate plants he does not like) and pesticides (products with which man is trying to eliminate insects and other small creatures that he doesn't like). It is only in the last three or four years that more than a minority of the populations of civilized countries have begun to suspect that those products will end up eliminating us. In non-civilized countries the natives have always suspected that anything capable of killing a plant or an insect could kill other beings as well.

The innocent cat is being affected by more than its fair share of these modern killers because it insists on keeping itself clean by meticulous licking, and because, given the opportunity, it will catch and eat insects. Obviously it will get a higher percentage of poisoned insects than healthy ones, and inevitably the percentage of toxins will build up within its body. Again, I include the following list primarily to help the reader learn what products are to be handled with the utmost care. I would at this point add two further cautions. Some manufacturers in their wisdom will call a common product by an uncommon name if the common product gets a bad name. Follow? Second, many products are combinations and the resultant symptoms may be rather confusing.

PETROLEUM PRODUCTS

The whole range from crude oil to paraffin is commonly used as vehicles for sprays and liquid poisons.

A cat may be liberally covered with the stuff without showing any symptoms whatsoever – at least for the first day or so. Nevertheless immediate home aid is essential. Otherwise the material will be absorbed and do permanent internal damage.

Using a mild detergent or green soap and many changes of warm water, wash as much off as you can. Then wrap the soggy creature in towels, put it in a basket, and go to the veterinarian.

ARSENIC

Most commonly used as an insect spray in orchards.

Symptoms include vomiting and extreme pain which soon results in weakness, collapse and death.

If you are sure of your diagnosis and if the poison has been recently taken you should try to induce vomiting. In the cat a heavy concentration of salt water, or mustard in water, or hydrogen peroxide often works. The antidote is B.A.L. (British Anti-Lewisite).

LIME AND SULPHUR

Commonly used as an orchard spray.

Usually the only symptoms are burns of the mouth caused by the lime.

Home aid includes a thorough washing of the mouth and the administration of a half teaspoon of milk of magnesia. Then to the veterinarian.

NICOTINE

Commonly used in plant sprays and in poultry houses.

Symptoms include vomiting, shivering fits, shaking, and a stiff staggering gait.

Early professional treatment is usually successful. It includes injections of stimulants and frequent gastric lavage. Home treatment is usually of no avail.

CHLORINATED HYDROCARBONS

This is the most ubiquitous group of insecticides and includes DDT; dieldrin; Aldrin; BHC; chlordane; TDE; toxaphene; and others. As the dealer said, 'Name your own poison.'

Symptoms include drooling, foaming at the mouth, shivering, tremors, and convulsions which lead to death.

Effective home aids include (a) the inducement of vomiting if several poisoned insects have been swallowed, followed by (b) the administration of some universal antidote or (c) a thorough washing with detergent or castile soap if the kitten has been accidentally sprayed and (d) a quarter grain of phenobarbitone if the kitten seems unduly nervous. Don't bother with any of those treatments if they will delay your trip to the veterinarian.

ORGANIC PHOSPHATES

Another large group of modern insecticides with such trade names as Demetion, TEPP, Parathion, EPN, and Malathion. Aside from Malathion (which may be used as a flea-killer on cats provided it is carefully brushed out) this group is deadly for cats.

Symptoms include drooling, abdominal pain, and convulsions which lead to death. One can differentiate this sort of poisoning from many others because of the excess watering of the eyes.

Even the mildest cases require professional treatment as soon as possible. Although it's not a specific antidote, atropine has saved many.

Another large group of dangerous substances is the antiseptics and disinfectants. Again, we must remember that if a substance is strong enough to kill a germ it must be able to harm our body cells. The most dangerous for cats are those that contain coal-tar products. They are phenols, or carbolic acid and its derivatives. They may do damage either by being swallowed or by being absorbed through the skin.

The symptoms include muscular convulsions followed by respiratory paralysis which leads to death.

If the cat is covered with the stuff wash it off. If the poison has been swallowed, induce vomiting and administer the universal antidote. Then to the veterinarian.

Kittens can get themselves coated in lead paint. And once, at our local R.S.P.C.A. Clinic, I was presented with a kitten that had been painted psychedelically by its infantile owners during a party. They were terribly amused until I told them that after I had treated the kitten I was going to institute a prosecution for cruelty to animals.

Symptoms include vomiting, drooling, muscular twitching, and walking in circles. Sometimes the cat will walk into a corner and stand there with its head against the wall. As the condition progresses convulsions occur, accompanied by violent involuntary chewing motions. Death usually ensues in twenty-four to thirty-six hours.

Home aid, of course, includes removing as much of the paint as possible. The specific antidote is called EDTA: Calcium disodiumethylenediamine tetracetate in 5 per cent glucose. This product combines with the lead in the system and renders it harmless.

Incidentally we cured the kitten and found it a suitable home, but we never did get to court because the people vanished.

Still another commonly used product that is very dangerous for cats is permanent-type anti-freeze containing ethylene glycol. Cats like the taste of it and kittens like it even more.

Symptoms include drowsiness, a staggering gait, paralysis of the hindquarters, and coma leading to death.

Treatment is usually unavailing, unless you actually catch

the kitten drinking the stuff and immediately induce vomiting. Then give the universal antidote.

PHILODENDRON

A very common household plant, containing a slow insidious poison.

A normal healthy playful kitten will turn into a dull listless thin one in a period of one to two months. The appetite becomes 'picky', there may be vomiting for no apparent reason and the kitten just seems to waste away. Quite often because of the undramatic course of the poisoning the owners will suspect worms and subject the unfortunate kitten to round after round of worm tablets and purgatives.

The only home aid is to remove the plant because quite often it will exert a fatal fascination for the kitten. The kitten should be hospitalized as soon as possible. Despite all treatment the mortality rate remains very high.

DIEFFENBACHIA

A household plant which causes acute poisoning.

Within seconds of eating the plant the kitten will exhibit signs of acute abdominal pain. It will roll on the floor and meow loudly. It will salivate profusely and spit out large quantities of foam.

First-aid is absolutely essential. Wrap the kitten in a towel with its head sticking out. Spoon down a teaspoonful of strong salt water solution or hydrogen peroxide or mustard water. If the green leaves don't come up repeat the procedure until they do. Then get the kitten to a veterinarian. If the kitten brings the leaves up within half an hour it has every chance of recovering. If they stay down for over an hour recovery is doubtful.

Dead and decaying leaves of many plants release cyanide. Fortunately, most taste unpleasant. Nevertheless some kittens will manage, in the enthusiasm of play, to swallow a fair bit.

Symptoms include heavy breathing which becomes short gasps before death.

Home aid includes emetics (salt water, mustard water or hydrogen peroxide) and afterwards the administration of methylene blue (dissolve a quarter of a cake of bluing used for washing in a pint of water and give two or three teaspoonfuls). Then to the veterinarian's.

LAUREL

Commonly grown in England and eastern America and frequently used as a part of a flower arrangement.

Symptoms include intense irritation and itchiness, drooling, running of the nose and eyes, followed by vomiting, stomach cramps, convulsions leading to death.

Home aid includes emetics, enemas, one quarter grain of phenobarbitone (if you can manage to get the tablet down without having your hand amputated) and warmth. Then to the veterinarian's. The mortality rate is very high.

MUSHROOMS AND TOADSTOOLS

Cats are quite as susceptible to the poisonous varieties of fungi as people.

Symptoms usually include drooling and vomiting leading to paralysis and death.

Home aid includes emetics to get rid of the stuff as soon as possible. Professional treatment includes atropine or belladonna depending on the symptoms.

There are two other very common sources of danger to the growing kitten. One is the motor-car. Kittens simply should not be allowed near traffic.

The other is children. Children should be told that Kitty may be played with gently but she is not to be carried about or dressed in costume, or placed in the refrigerator or washing machine. She is not to be painted. Objects are not to be tied to her tail; nor may chewing gum be put in her ears. One must not give Kitty a haircut, nor cut her with a knife or hit her with a hammer. One should not push her off the roof nor hang her from a tree. One shouldn't soak her in petrol and set her on fire. Nor should one throw her across the fence to the neighour's dogs. Kitty should not be thrown into a scalding bath and she shouldn't be flushed down the toilet.

Do you think all those things are improbable? Once upon a time I might have thought so too. Twenty-odd years of veterinary practice have taught me otherwise.

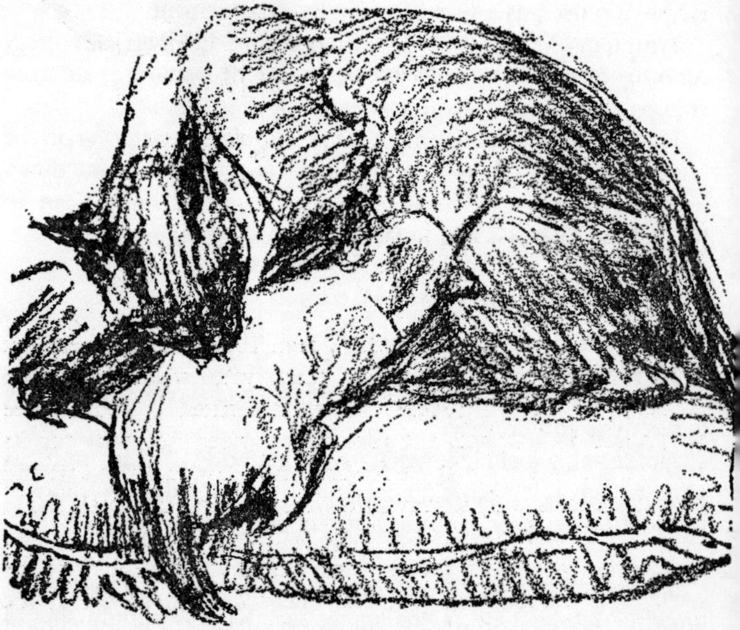

4 The Weanling Kitten

During the first two weeks the queen constantly mothers her kittens. She nuzzles and licks them into wakefulness and encourages them to suckle. When the kitten is about three weeks old it first gets the idea that it need not wait for its mother to announce that it's feeding time. Gradually at first and then more insistently it shows that it is learning the harsh lesson of life! You don't get anything without asking for it, and quite often you don't get anything unless you take it. It is the magnet of the mother's teat that draws the kittens out of the nest to take their first faltering exploratory steps.

At first these forays are short and hesitant. And they are quickly aborted by a headlong rushed return should a sudden noise or a suspicious odour or a strange sight intrude. Those forays outside the nest area become constantly longer. The short minutes during which the kittens forget themselves sufficiently to bound away from their mother become longer minutes in which they play with each other and explore their surroundings.

Many lessons need to be learned. Kittens practise hunting each other. They test the possibilities of camouflage by trying to merge with the background before the attack. They try to make themselves even more difficult to spot by freezing into immobility the moment the 'prey' looks in their direction. They practise crawling in a crouched position so as to attract less attention. They learn how far they are able to pounce with efficiency and hence how close they must get to the 'prey'.

They learn the limits of their strength and speed in play-fights with their mates and their mother. And very quickly they learn one of the most important lessons of all, which is to vanish at the slightest sign of danger.

During the first week or week and a half of these brave confrontations with the new world outside the nest, the mother initiates much of the play and is either tolerant or positively benevolent about the rest. At four to five weeks of age – depending upon size and individuals and numbers – the mother begins to avoid the kittens for longer and longer periods. We don't know whether she does this unconsciously because evolution favours kittens that learn independence early, or for the much more prosaic reason that her nipples are getting sore. We do know that the time she actually spends nursing her litter steadily declines. By the time the kittens are five weeks old she is spending less than five hours a day nursing them.

And it is when they are about five weeks of age that the weaning process properly begins. It is at that age that average kittens in normal conditions begin to take more than a curious interest in solid food. By the end of the fifth week most kittens are eagerly seeking it.

It is at this stage that the kittens learn the difference between hunting as play and hunting as a serious occupation. Some studies show that kittens whose mother bring home half-dead rodents for them to kill are more likely to grow into hunters than those whose mothers do not display their killing prowess.

From the fifth week onward the kittens will follow the mother for considerable distances. If the mother is a hunter the kittens will follow her on her hunting trips. And, as you might expect, such kittens too are more likely to grow into hunters and predators than those whose mothers restrict their foraging to the closest refrigerator.

In this context there are two other results of studies that are worth reporting. The first is that kittens raised with rats or mice tend to play with them – as if they were litter mates – rather than hunt them as normally raised cats do. The second is that kittens raised in a normal environment by hunting mothers but fed on a vegetarian diet grow into hunters every bit as avid as those raised on a meat diet. The 'vegetarian' kittens, however, tend to eat the results of the hunt less frequently. Hunger did not seem to make members of either group more anxious to hunt or to kill. These apparently confusing results confirm that both hunting and killing are partly learned and partly instinctive in the cat, and that both are often 'enjoyed' for their own sake. Is that 'enjoyment' a form of play? It is thought not. Play might be defined as a pretence of hunting or killing. It is a preparation and learning for the real thing. Play is an exuberant activity without immediate serious purpose, which can be easily interrupted; a serious task, on the other hand, is never interrupted by play.

Under natural conditions, which I suppose we can take as meaning on the farms and in the warehouses, the kittens' first introduction to solid food is, as I said, the rats or mice which their mother carries home. Later they learn about such delights as flies and other insects (pray God there's less DDT than fly) and if it's springtime the culls and fledglings fallen from their nests (pray God the same). We who have assumed responsibility for our cats, however, may not and must not accept that sort of fortuitous diet as being in any sense satisfactory. In fact cats that live on a diet of rodents frequently waste away through constant vomiting caused by the irritating agents in hides and tails. Surely an advanced society demands that any person too poor in purse or in spirit to care for his animals properly shall not be allowed to keep them.

What *is* an ideal diet for the weanling kitten? Let me outline the ingredients using nutritional terms, pointing out as I go the more common deficiencies and pitfalls.

The most important part of the diet of higher animals – and that includes even the lowliest of cats – is water. There are many recorded instances of people, cattle, dogs, and cats that have survived weeks of starvation. After a few days without water, however, life fades.

Many cat owners swear by their honour (some will even wager good money) that their cat defies all biological law and could survive a Schweppesless summer in the Sahara. They fail to realize just how much water is contained in ordinary food. Fresh vegetables, for example, contain 70 to 80 per cent water. Even the so-called dried ones contain 15 to 20 per cent water. Fat meat contains 40 per cent water. Lean meat contains 55 to 60 per cent water. Many cats get their water requirements from milk, which is 87 per cent water. And just in case you wondered how Mr Thermodor, the cat food manufacturer, manages to maintain his lovely red complexion despite his wife's appalling gambling losses, let me remind you that many tinned foods contain as much as 90 per cent water.

As a general rule a kitten on a moist ration requires about a tablespoonful of water a day. As it matures its requirement will increase. Most adult cats on a moist ration get along with about three tablespoonfuls of water a day. A cat on a dry ration, living in a drying centrally heated atmosphere, might require as much as seven times that amount.

Some of us become infuriated when our cats turn up their noses at our genuine hand-turned pottery bowl in order to slink out and dip a dainty tongue into the mud puddle in the back alley.

Why do so many cats prefer not to drink at home? Their sense of taste hasn't become jaded. Given the opportunity they prefer outdoor water, even if it's only the collected drips from the roof, to water that contains added chemicals. I wonder too if their sensitive tongues can tell how many times our ordinary tap water has been through the sewage plant.

Be that as it may, many cats have to content themselves with tap water. The least we can do is to make sure it's relatively fresh by changing it two or three times a day. Should the bowl become dusty it should be cleaned and thoroughly rinsed. Remember too that many cats would rather not drink from a bowl into which a dog has slobbered. Don't you find that understandable?

The next most important part of the diet is the protein group. These are the substances which the body uses to build new tissue or to repair the old tissues. Youth is the time of building and age is the time of repair. Young kittens require approximately 32 per cent protein. A grown cat of middle years can get along on 22 per cent. Later on as he mellows his requirements will jump to 32 per cent again. Those are percentages of the dry weight of the ration. Few tinned foods – particularly the cheaper sorts made for dogs – contain even half the amount of protein. Hence they are unsuitable for the growing kitten. They are best reserved for those long weekends when the butcher shop is shut.

The most commonly available and the most commonly used source of protein is the fresh and internal organs of other animals and birds and fish. Other sources include eggs, soyabeans, alfalfa meal, and cheese. Ordinary cow's milk is not quite rich enough – you must use undiluted condensed milk or powdered milk mixed to twice the strength you would use for feeding a human baby.

Yet another category of food is the carbohydrate group. These are the starches and the sugars. We human beings eat them in order to get energy. Some of us don't need any energy so we eat sugars and starches in order to get fat. Cats don't utilize carbohydrates very well. They will, however, eat starches if they have been well cooked. They enjoy spaghetti, boiled beans, and potatoes, for example. Although these dishes don't do any harm, the cat won't get much nutritive value from them. They are useful primarily as a change, a treat, and as bulk-makers in the diet of patients suffering from kidney conditions.

The cat's body is better able to obtain its energy by metabolizing that group of food stuffs known as fats. That group is also necessary for building muscle and nerve tissue. There are two general types of fats – saturated or animal fats, and unsaturated or vegetable fats and oils. The diet should include both. Fat meat should be fed at least once a week. Corn oil or margarine should be fed three times a week. The growing kitten will need about a third of a teaspoonful at a feeding whereas the adult will want a whole teaspoonful. Cod liver oil is also a good form of animal fat, but only a high grade should be used. An adult cat can have a teaspoonful twice a week; half that amount is sufficient for a kitten.

The fat of red tuna and rancid oils cause a disease known as steatis or yellow fat disease. I'm sorry I didn't tell you that before you bought a whole case of tuna. All is not lost however – you can eat it yourself!

Yet another important group of food stuffs is the minerals. Although there are at least nine that are essential for cats, for all practical purposes we need only pay attention to four. The others (sodium chloride, potassium, manganese, zinc, and cobalt) are found in adequate quantities in most average cat diets.

We must, however, give a little thought to calcium, phosphorus, iron, and iodine. The first two work together. An excess or deficiency of either will result in sore legs and joints, poor teeth, and malformed bones.

All sorts of creatures suffer either deficiency or imbalance of calcium and phosphorus because people simply do not realize that meat does not contain sufficient quantities of either. Milk and eggs are a good source of both but quite often the weanling kitten will need supplements as well. The best form is, of course, natural ground bone meal. Make sure you buy the feeding bone meal, not the sort that one uses in the garden. Usually about a half teaspoonful a day is all that is needed for a growing kitten.

Your veterinarian may prefer to dispense a vitamin mineral supplement. Although these are more expensive they are properly balanced for other elements besides calcium and phosphorus and if used as directed trace deficiencies are unlikely to occur. There is no reason whatsoever why those tablets shouldn't be properly labelled. A kitten needs 300 mgms a day of calcium and 200 mgms of phosphorus, and in about that ratio.

A most dramatic deficiency condition, which we veterinarians incorrectly term Osteogenesis Imperfecta, is seen not uncommonly in Oriental cats and occasionally in other sorts as well. The scientists are still arguing about what the condition should properly be called.

Affected kittens suffer with multiple fractures. A sudden jar, a three-inch drop, or a violent movement is sufficient to fracture a bone. One Burmese I remember was brought into the clinic because, as its owner said, 'It stays in one position! It absolutely refuses to move.' We X-rayed the kitten and found that it had over twenty separate fractures! Response to treatment is usually dramatic, and that kitten surprised his owner and pleased us by proving no exception to the rule. Like many Orientals it simply refused milk. And unlike most Orientals it refused cheese and eggs as well. We mixed natural bone meal with its meat, we shoved some vitamin mineral pills down its throat, and we gave injections of calcium, phosphorus, and vitamin D. Within forty-eight hours the kitten attempted a few tentative movements in the direction of its litter tray. At the end of seventy-two hours, slowly and painfully, it made it. At the end of the first week further X-rays showed that the bones were knitting nicely and the kitten was sent home with piles of bone meal and stacks of pills and the owner was warned that the kitten had to be confined to a small area not much larger than an apple box for a further ten days. After that the kitten resumed a normal life.

And just in case you think veterinary surgeries are unromantic places let me tell you that the owner of that kitten met a gentleman from British Guiana (now Guyana) in the waiting room. Subsequently they married and in due course I granted an export certificate for her Burmese and his whippet and off they went to the Rampanuni. Where, according to their Christmas cards, they live happily ever after.

Iron is found mainly in meat, liver, and kidney. A kitten needs only about five mgms a day. As it's used in the formation of haemoglobin, a deficiency results in anaemia. It occurs most commonly in kittens that are fed on an exclusive milk and cereal diet. Again, treatment almost always brings about a dramatic improvement. An injection or two of iron and a few tablets of the same turns Tired Pastellina into Energetic Rosie.

Iodine is necessary for the proper functioning of the thyroid gland. This is the gland that controls growth and metabolism. A deficiency of iodine results in stunted growth and a dull starey coat. A pregnant cat that doesn't get sufficient iodine may produce deformed kittens.

Most of us in inland areas buy iodized salt. Hence iodine deficiency, both in ourselves and in our cats, is becoming increasingly uncommon. We may also get adequate amounts of iodine from seafoods. Pilchards, sardines, and pink salmon are nutritionally little different from sole, lobster, or sturgeon. You can tell your husband that next time he complains. He must know perfectly well that you can't afford to buy lobster for every creature in the house and there's hardly any point in keeping a kitten if one is not prepared to look after it properly.

The final group of food stuffs the cat owner must consider is the vitamins. These, like the proteins, are important during all the stages of a cat's life, but are particularly so during periods of stress, during pregnancy and lactation, and at the two extremes of age.

Vitamin A, also known as carotene or the yellow vitamin (because it is found in most yellow vegetables, such as carrots and corn), is also sometimes called the ophthalmic or anti-infectivity vitamin, and for good reason. The first symptoms of a vitamin A deficiency are often sore runny eyes with a reddish discharge, often followed by a sore throat or a cold.

The reddish discharge from the eyes is almost always a certain sign of vitamin A deficiency. If neglected the eye itself will start to dry out after forty-eight or seventy-two hours. Not unnaturally the kitten will become very sensitive to light and will prefer to stay hidden.

Kittens suffering from a milder form of deficiency will not show such dramatic signs. They will be more susceptible to infection, and they will grow more slowly than kittens fed on an adequate, varied, well supplemented diet.

Many adult cats suffer a vitamin A deficiency without showing any dramatic or even obvious signs. Some queens may have long periods between heats. Some may even stop coming into season. Toms will have a reduced interest in queens. Those that are aroused prove to have poor sperm development. Some queens that conceive lose their kittens early. Some kittens born will be small, weak, and often deformed. And some of the kittens may appear normal at birth but within a month or six weeks develop abnormalities such as enlarged heads, weak hips, and palsy.

May I at this point again remind my readers that this book is not a substitute for professional treatment. Its greatest value may lie in its usefulness as a guide to the urgency of that treatment. If your kitten has a painful red discharge from its eyes please don't say to yourself, 'Oh that's quite obviously a deficiency of vitamin A, I can cure that myself.' It may well be. But if it isn't, that kitten will suffer unnecessarily while you postpone a visit to your veterinarian.

Professional treatment of advanced cases of vitamin A deficiency in the kitten or the aged cat will include injections and instillation directly into the eyes of a concentrated form of cod liver oil known as Oleum Percomorpheum.

Suckling and weanling kittens should be given cod liver oil two or three times a week. You may gauge the high level of vitamin A necessary for health in the cat by the fact that most one-a-day vitamin tablets for humans contain approximately a thousand units of vitamin A, while the cat requires approximately twice that much. Many breeders find it more convenient, if slightly more expensive, to give a drop a day of Oleum Percomorpheum. And although I hesitate to name a commercial preparation as a recommendation I must mention that Abidec drops have earned a deserved reputation in the nutrition of growing kittens, supplying them with adequate amounts of both vitamin A and D. Slightly cheaper but not so convenient are many of the vitamin–mineral supplement pills available.

Adult cats that receive two meals a week of liver, raw or cooked, seldom need any vitamin A supplement.

The vitamin B group includes B_1, B_2, B_6 and niacin, all of which are found in adequate quantities in uncooked meat. A deficiency of vitamin B may result in a variety of symptoms, including twitching of the muscles of the face, a dull coat, general weakness, ulcers of the mouth and even convulsions. We see those symptoms regularly in kittens that are fed an exclusively cooked diet. We almost never see a deficiency in kittens fed a variety of raw or slightly cooked meats.

Manufacturers of tinned foods for cats know that cooking destroys thiamin, and the conscientious ones add this vitamin after cooking. However, it is still wise to supplement the diets of those cats so unfortunate to live on a tinned food with a couple of tablets a day of ordinary brewer's yeast. It is cheap and most cats enjoy the taste so much that they will eat them much as children eat sweets. Their very palatability has made these tablets very popular throughout the cat-keeping world. Manufacturers advertise them as being the answer to all a cat's problems, and the gullible public buys them at inflated prices because 'Puss wouldn't eat them if they weren't good for her.' Some people reason that if two are good fifteen or twenty are better. Others wonder and feel their faith shaking when Kitty gets flu or worms or mange despite the fact that she is getting her full quota of those wonderful pills. I fully expect someone to bring in a cat with a broken leg and ask me how such an injustice could have occurred to a cat that has never missed her daily quota.

Vitamin D, also known as calciferol or the sunshine vitamin, helps the body to properly utilize calcium and phosphorus in the manufacture of strong healthy bones and teeth. Whole summer milk, fresh eggs, and irradiated evaporated milk are all good sources of vitamin D, and so is cod liver oil. Use that or its concentrated forms or substitutes as outlined for vitamin A.

There are other vitamins and vitamin-like factors that are necessary for the maintenance of good health in most animals. These include vitamin E (also known as alpha tocopherol) vitamin K, biotin, inositol, vitamin B_2, and choline. In day-to-day practice a deficiency of those vitamins never seems to cause any trouble. It may be that the deficiencies of other vitamins show up earlier or it may be that the cat's requirements for these vitamins is not so high as it is for those I have discussed in detail. Manufacturers of cat foods and vitamin and mineral supplements prefer not to take a chance. They include the lot. At least the conscientious ones do.

I hope all those nutritional facts don't prove too indigestible. Now to translate them into a practical feeding programme for the weanling kitten.

If the mother has a great deal of milk she might allow the kittens to continue suckling for as long as eight or ten or even twelve weeks. Under certain circumstances the kittens will keep suckling for considerably longer. It is not entirely unknown, for example, for a kitten to keep suckling her mother until she herself is almost ready to give birth.

Sometimes a kitten that has been weaned from its mother for several weeks, and subsequently is sold to a new home, will without fuss or ceremony join a nursing litter. I know one Abyssinian that was purchased at four months, five weeks after it had been weaned. In the new home was a Siamese queen with lots of milk and only four kittens. As the Siamese kittens were only two weeks old one might have thought that that additional mouth at the fountain was not only unfair but undignified, but the mother didn't think so. She appeared to welcome the stranger as a kind of bonus, and even spent many more minutes every day industriously grooming the newcomer than she did her own kittens. One cynical observer suggested that her real interest was in licking those stripes off to reveal a Siamese purity below.

There are many other variations on the nursing–weanling theme. The point is if a kitten is getting adequate amounts of milk from its own mother or from another nursing cat it's hardly likely to go crazy with desire if you walk by with a quart of standardized homogenized pasteurized milk fresh from the refrigerator. Why should it? It is only we superior humans who have been conditioned into preferring the milk of the cow to all others.

Theoretically kittens are weaned from the mother to a half dozen daily meals of which three are milk or milk and cereal, and the other three are meat. In practice it seldom works that way. Almost always the kittens will prefer to keep having their three or four or five daily milk meals from their mother while sampling meat between times. That seems to accord with the dictates of both nature and common sense (almost always they are one and the same thing).

Whenever the kittens start to show an interest in solid food (by sampling their mother's bowl or the spoils of her hunt) you may begin the gradual process of weaning by offering meals of any of the two or three dozen acceptable forms of protein.

If the kittens devour chicken breast with gusto but merely pick at ground sirloin of beef, don't make the mistake of offering only chicken thereafter. It is during the weanling stage that eating habits, good or bad, are established. If the kittens refuse a particular item skip it for two or three days, but don't scrub it from the list of possible variations. Try it again a few days later. They may still not be very enthusiastic but you can be sure that at least one Georgie the Gorger will dig in and the others, motivated more by curiosity and jealousy than hunger, will follow suit.

The choice is wide. Kittens will survive and thrive on the entire bodies of insects, small birds, small rodents, or on the flesh of almost any large living creature whether fish, fowl, or beast. Generally it is best not to depend entirely on the hunting prowess of the mother or her brood. Nor are many of us gentle catlovers able or inclined to do our own killing. We prefer to leave that activity to the butcher, the fishmonger, and their suppliers.

Aside from pork, which seems to upset some kittens, practically everything those gentlemen sell is suitable. Most kittens do well on raw chopped lean beef. Veal, lamb and mutton, fish and chicken tend to be rather laxative in effect unless cooked. Remember that cooking may destroy all or part of their Vitamin B, so supplement with brewer's yeast. Bones, particularly tiny splintery cooked ones, must be removed.

Here are a couple of dozen different menus that successful breeders of my acquaintance have used during the weaning process: Roast lamb (not overdone, the fat removed, coarsely chopped); beef or lamb liver (raw if the kittens are slightly constipated, otherwise lightly cooked, sliced in slivers); chicken livers (boiled and sliced); ox or lamb kidney (grilled and sliced); fowl (boiled or roasted, boned and flaked or torn into bits); salmon (pink or red, tinned or more expensive); sardines; white fish (fresh or frozen, cooked, boned, and flaked); best quality tinned or bottled baby food (beef, veal, chicken, or turkey); best quality tinned cat food (not more than three or four meals a week); ox tongue (boiled and sliced); horse meat (fresh or frozen, roasted or boiled, chopped); turkey (leftover or otherwise, roasted, boned, and chopped); frankfurters (don't repeat if they cause the runs); pheasant (don't laugh! I know lots of places where it's cheaper than chicken, roasted, boned, and chopped); leftovers; handouts; offerings and droppings from the table (definitely not recommended as it's a difficult habit to break); and many etceteras.

Do you get the idea? Almost any vegetable (except potato peelings) raw or cooked may be added in very small quantities. And don't forget to get them used to the yeast tablets, the cod liver oil, or the combined vitamin–mineral tablets from an early stage.

Some nursing cats cannot provide milk sufficient for the kittens' needs beyond three and a half to four weeks of age. Others don't taper off until six or seven weeks or later. You can tell easily enough because kittens that aren't getting sufficient milk from their mothers will accept the substitute you provide. Many people find that the most convenient milk for weanlings is the top third of unhomogenized whole milk from Jerseys, Guernseys, or Ayrshires. That portion seems to agree with many kittens, although it is much richer as regards fat but poorer in solids than cat's milk. Another commonly used formula is powdered whole milk, reconstituted to twice the strength recommended for human babies. Undiluted tinned milk is also acceptable, and some people find that they can get away with using ordinary cow's milk. As it's not nearly rich enough for the needs of the growing kitten, kittens weaned to such a mixture often do not develop as rapidly or as well as their better-fed mates. And finally there are some very good commercial powdered formulae on the market. They are specially formulated to replace the milk of the mother cat and they are well worth the price.

Practically all the articles I've ever read on weaning kittens state that to the milk mixture should be added a high quality baby cereal. In my experience a high percentage of kittens, despite all one's wiles, will refuse the whole meal if cereal has been added. Give it a try and prove me wrong!

Many kittens, however, will accept eggs in almost any form in one of their daily milk meals. Others will accept a mixture of one of those wonderful new completely balanced biscuit foods. After a few introductions with the milk many kittens become enthusiastic about those foods in their dry form.

Again, Orientals provide a special problem. Once they leave their mothers many of them never again taste milk. Some can be persuaded to eat enough eggs, cheese, yoghurt, and other dairy products to get the necessary vitamins and minerals. Others may have to get the supplements previously mentioned, either mixed with their meat meals or forcibly fed.

Gradually the kittens look to their mothers less and their bowls more. Weaning is a slow undramatic affair, or at least should be.

We veterinarians commonly get asked the following four questions about cat husbandry during the weanling period. Firstly, how much should one actually feed? There is no hard-and-fast rule. A big-boned kitten born of a long line of back alley bruisers might easily consume two or three times as much as an Oriental kitten of the same age. If you buy one ounce of solid food for every pound of growing kitten per day you won't find yourself with a lot of leftovers. Nor will the kittens be unduly hungry.

If, for example, the litter is composed of six kittens each

weighing about a pound and a half you'll know that throughout the day they'll require approximately a half pound of food. If they're getting a fair bit of milk from their mother they'll obviously need less. If they're playing a lot in the chill outdoors they may require a bit more. If they're leaving a lot of it or if they devour it all in a few short seconds and scream for more you'd better get out the computer and feed it a new set of facts.

Another common query is, 'They've refused a meal. Should I rush them round to the hospital?'

If they appear bright and are still active and playing, the answer is No. If, on the other hand, they're just lying about and appear indifferent or if they've skipped two or three meals in a row then they'd better be seen by the veterinarian.

Yet a third common question is 'They've got the runs. What do I do?'

The veterinarian will usually want to know if in fact the whole litter has diarrhoea. Quite often only a single adventurous kitten has sampled the dregs of a frying pan or the butt of a cigarette. If so it will be making frequent trips to the litter tray, where much of its straining will be unproductive. Give it a charcoal tablet or two, starve it for a dozen hours, and in most cases it will bounce right back to health.

If the whole litter is involved you'd better cast your mind back over the previous twenty-four-hour regime. Have you changed the milk formula? Was it fresh? Properly mixed? Refrigerated promptly? Warmed to slightly above room temperature? Were all the feeding dishes properly cleaned? Disinfected and rinsed? Are you sure? Think again! Remember milk in all its forms is an ideal medium for bacterial growth. How about the solid foods?

The safest home aid is ten or twelve hours of starvation. A common (but uncommonly good) commercial white preparation available on both sides of the Atlantic is called Kaopectate. It is good for man, beast and woman. I've never heard of it doing any harm and it often does a lot of good. Give between one quarter of a teaspoonful and a whole teaspoonful to each kitten depending on its size. Repeat three or four times a day. You'll find that after one day of using this medicine the walls of a fair-sized room will be covered with it. If the kittens aren't better by the next day take them along to your veterinarian. Why do you think he paints his walls white?

'One of them brought up a worm. Shall I dose the lot?' is another common inquiry. Most veterinarians will want you to save the worm, because different sorts require different kinds of treatment. They'll also want to know the exact ages and weights of your kittens. Kittens may be seriously harmed by indiscriminate worming. Please don't do it except under veterinary supervision.

What else happens during this stage of kittenhood? The lessons of house training are learned to perfection. Most kittens learn to use a toilet area or tray almost as they emerge from the nest. Within the nest their mother's fastidiousness and constant grooming will have impressed them. And outside they'll get a clout should they squat in an unapproved place. But they're young and they will make mistakes. Sometimes a sleepy kitten will forget to concentrate and his aim will stray from target. Sometimes in the middle of a vigorous game he will realize that he's behind schedule. The last few feet of his frantic rush to the tray may be accompanied by a certain amount of undignified spillage. One must be tolerant of these mishaps. They may occur fairly frequently during the third week and occasionally into the fourth week but by the time the kitten is two months of age those episodes will be but smelly memories. The only other domesticated creature which is so naturally clean is the pig.

If you intend your kittens to be well behaved members of other households you owe it to the kittens and to their future sponsors to begin their 'people education' during this transitional stage of their lives. For example, kittens must be taught to accept grooming by humans. This needn't be a complicated or time-consuming business. In the case of Orientals and short-haired breeds you simply run a brush or a soft cloth over their coats. Long-haired cats will have to be combed. Have a look at the ears. They may have those telltale black deposits which mean earmites. Wipe away any discharge from the eyes. Sometimes undue straining is caused by a lump of dried faeces under the tail. Wash it away gently.

Kittens are allowed the odd idle scratch. If they scratch a great deal, however, it's time to institute a flea hunt. If a kitten spends minute after long minute licking at a particular paw have a look and see if it has trodden in some chewing gum. Gently remove it. That's what grooming is all about.

'People' training should also include kitchen manners. Kittens are not meant to walk across tables. Nor are they meant to beg underfoot. Stealing should be punished. How do you punish a cat? By expressing displeasure either verbally in loud harsh tones or by a gentle sharp slap across the flanks. The important principle of punishment is that it be inflicted exactly at the time of the offence. One lady I know spent several hours baking a fourteen-pound salmon. She allowed it to cool in the cooking juices and she then decorated it lavishly with green and red peppers delicately carved to represent eyes, fins, and markings. Then she went to the hairdresser's to prepare for the festive evening ahead. When she arrived home she found the peppers. The fish, however, had gone. Furious, she stomped around the house until she came upon her big Manx queen benignly watching her large litter playing football with a spool of thread. I don't know what the good lady said to the mother cat and her kittens but I'm told that never again did any of them feel at ease with a spool of thread. All of them however, retain a rather sophisticated taste in fish.

It is quite simple to teach kittens not to scratch anything except a post which you provide especially for that purpose. Each and every time a kitten tries to sharpen its claws on your Chesterfield or on the leg of your teak dining-room table (eighteen more payments before it's yours) you must gently pick it up and place it by the scratching post. The system works pretty well, provided you have several assistants and only one kitten.

One friend of mine, an airline pilot, married a lady with two entire Siamese queens. During the honeymoon he brought back some rolls of exquisite silk from Thailand which he proudly had affixed to the walls of his dining-room. A year later he said to me, 'After the second litter I reconciled myself to losing the wall covering shred by shred. My mistake was, that when Pam said I'd be lucky if they left the walls I thought she was joking.'

You should provide toys for the growing litter that have no opportunity to learn by hunting. Ping-pong balls provide hours of amusement and reflex sharpening. Unlike many other balls and marbles, they are not easily swallowed, and they're too light to chip a tooth. Tunnels of cardboard or of wood through which the kittens may crawl and in which they may hide if they are so inclined are also safe and amusing. What lessons they teach I cannot imagine. Any object suspended from the ceiling constitutes for the kitten an invitation for tennis for one.

I think rubber and plastic mice are boring and so do most kittens after a few moments. Of one thing I'm sure. I have yet to meet a kitten so stupid as to be misled into believing that one of those objects bore any resemblance to a rodent alive or dead. Any interest they may exhibit is due solely to their strangeness, their bounciness, or the catnip with which some of them are impregnated. Generally speaking it is best not to offer plastic or rubber toys to the weanling kitten. Neither of those substances is digestible. Either, if stuck inside, may cause a fatal obstruction.

But of course, as any child can tell you, the best sort of play is that which is shared with another living creature. Fortunate indeed is the kitten that when finally fully weaned from its mother goes to a new home with at least one of its brothers or sisters. I can think of no disadvantage (aside from additional expense) from the owner's point of view in acquiring new kittens two at a time. The advantages, however, are many and obvious.

Next to another kitten of about the same age the most ideal playmate may well be a recently weaned puppy. Provided you are vigilant through the first three or four days of introduction, and provided the one that got there first gets a bit of additional fuss, they soon learn not only to respect but to actively enjoy each other. Aside from some of the more aggressive terriers there are few breeds of dog that don't settle into a comfortable and mutually comforting relationship with cats. I even know many hounds that are rampaging killers of any strange creature but absolutely adore the cat on the home hearth. And many children who are gentle enough, sensible enough, and considerate enough to gain the confidence of a newly weaned kitten may spend hour upon hour and day after day in profitable physical and verbal intercommunication with their furry friend.

Ideally the kitten should be almost unaware of his gradual weaning and removal to a new home. Almost imperceptibly at about seven or eight or nine weeks of age the nursing sessions taper into a perfunctory ritual. The kitten still follows the mother about, but more in the expectation of a successful hunt than for liquid refreshment.

The mother for her part becomes increasingly bored with the kittens and suffers them less gladly. Between seven and ten weeks of age, depending on local conditions, the kittens should receive inoculation against feline infectious enteritis. Recommendations for further jabs will be made by your local veterinarian. The immunity obtained from an injection while the kitten is still on the mother is often not as strong as that obtained when the injection is given much later. But as the kitten who is still with his mother appears to get over those injections much quicker the disadvantage isn't great, particularly if the veterinarian uses a vaccine which will be repeated a couple or three weeks after full weaning.

When the kitten goes to its new home you should take an additional ten or fifteen minutes to sit down and explain to the new owners both verbally and in writing exactly the routine that has been followed. Put down feeding times. Put down sleeping times. Show them the kind of dishes you have been using and how you've cleaned and rinsed them. Show them the kitten's bed. Write down a full and complete diet for at least one week. And write down the name of your veterinarian.

Did the new owners come equipped with a cat basket? If

not why not? Are they going to be willing to provide proper fresh food at least five days of the week? Are they going to leave the kitten alone all day and every day from day one? Do they intend keeping the kitten in a cold garage or in an unheated cellar?

You must remember that many people buy a kitten as if it were a piece of merchandise. Either the children have blackmailed them into agreeing or they're the kind of oafs who wish to impress or keep up with their neighbours. These are often the sort of people who will get rid of the kitten as soon as it proves to be a bother or will conveniently allow it to become lost. Don't be afraid of acting like a crackpot. Put them through a regular inquisition. If they're genuine they won't mind and if they're not, your kitten has been spared a visit to hell.

If you think I exaggerate, how would you describe it if you were moved from a comfortable home and the creatures you've always known and placed in a cold dark place and given a bowl of foul-smelling mush? How would you describe it if you couldn't find the proper toilet area in your new unfamiliar surroundings and finally after many hours of restraint you couldn't contain yourself any longer whereupon a strange person came along and struck you sharply and pushed you out into the rainy outdoors until morning?

In my experience there are two very simple ways of avoiding such tragedies. First, one should never give a kitten away. Even if you don't want any money for it yourself insist that the new owners there and then send a cheque to the R.S.P.C.A. I don't know why it is but people will care for something that they've paid for whereas they think that something free is of no value. Second, impress upon the prospective owners that you will be willing to take the kitten back within the week. Tell them that all they need do is phone you and you'll go and get it.

One breeder of my acquaintance gives the purchaser twenty stamped self-addressed postcards.

'I want a progress report every two months for the first year and every year thereafter,' says she, 'and if I don't get one I'll pray that you'll come to an evil end.' She's a formidable-looking lady with one eye that slants upwards and she tells me that never has a postcard gone astray.

Most people will be only too appreciative of your help and advice in helping the newest member of the family settle in. After all, for ten years or more that furry creature will be adding another dimension to their lives.

Within days of its arrival it will have managed to fill every corner of the house and insinuate itself into every conversation and situation. It takes a few days longer for the new owners to realize that the ownership of their property is gradually passing into feline paws.

A kitten that has been weaned from her mother to six daily feeds will be down to four by the time she is four months old. A month later and she will be satisfied with three – but each will be a substantial meal. She will still require approximately an ounce of food for every pound she weighs, but as these fourth and fifth months are periods of rapid growth, the total amount fed will exactly double during the period.

Almost imperceptibly, at least to those who live with her, the kitten develops and changes. And almost overnight, it seems, the kitten of yesterday begins assuming the dimensions and attitudes of an adult.

Then one morning she begins to act strangely. Could it be? Surely not! But she's hardly six months old. Nevertheless it's happening. Oh my goodness! My cat's in love. What'll I do?

Index